BEST
APOCALYPSE
EVER

James True

Dedicated to Josh Crooklyn.
#KeepingItCrooklyn

CHAPTER ONE

American Leviathan

"They came with a Bible and their religion, stole our land, crushed our spirit, and now they tell us we should be thankful to the Lord for being saved." - Chief Pontiac

We pay reverence to the laminated credential. We trade our elders for politicians. We demonize the word savage to anoint the word civil. We trade tribe for town, horse for train, and brave for meek. We put a bounty on the scalp of every Indian and buffalo. We declare land's rape an offering to manifest destiny. The natives of America called this affliction wetiko. It's an addiction to the taste for something predictable. We sacrifice our spirit for a hook to hang our vigilance.

The New World Order is an Old World Order and that's why it's so hard to see. America was conquered, not found. Many nations participated in eradicating a thriving culture and people. Wetiko congealed into the American Leviathan. Its body filled the empty chambers of men and their institutions. Its shape reflects the fear and fetish of its organs. We are the pancreas of Babylon digesting everything she swallows. From Wounded Knee to Waco, she never learns from a mistake. Only now do we realize she never made one. Babylon is perfect.

Babylon is a thriving leviathan. We are swimming in the warm venom of its possession. We cannibalize our feet to combat a fear of standing. Crazy Horse stood tall when they stabbed him in the back. Sitting Bull was shot in the head by his people. Spotted Elk was gunned down by the army charged to protect him. Geronimo died a war prisoner of the land he defended. These are American saints double-crossed and crucified with nails of lead. These are the elders of American soil and we amputated their history.

Before there was America there was A-Mu-Ra-Ca, the land of the plumed serpent. In Central America, Columbus discovered natives from the north who called themselves Americos. History is obliterated by Babylon's soothings. Heritage becomes a precious commodity we smuggle underground. Civilization hunts it down like a miner sweeping his footprints from a cave. We create government to bury secrets too painful to tell. We all know what happened to the giants. They are crouching inside us, waiting for us to be brave.

In the first colonies of America, it was illegal to join the natives. You were shot and killed for integrating with the soil or its people. Civilization renames a land to own it. It erases its identity like kidnapped children. Your name is North Carolina. We will call you Georgia. Civilization tells you it is wrong to possess the feathers of eagle, hawk, or owl. It tells their citizens to kill fox, raccoon, skunk, or groundhog. Civilization says all of its children are tainted by disease. Civilization cleanses its children with tiny daggers dipped in vaccine. Civilization says its children may not feed from the river without a credential.

Only man can put himself on his knees. Several years before the Civil War, there was massive recruitment of northern armies mustered to exterminate sovereignty throughout the south. By this time, nearly one third of the Eastern Cherokee were white men. Nearly half of the Seminole tribe was black. The Indian word "Creek" means wild or runaway. Integration had been happening naturally by bioregion. As the French became Cherokee and Huron, Pilgrims were outlawing long hair to stop the emptying of their villages. The Roanoke Colony abandoned England to merge with the Croatan. Hernando De Soto posted permanent guards to keep his villagers from defecting. This was a problem for the monarchies, as more settlers were joining the natives. Ben Franklin wrote, "No European who has tasted Savage Life can afterwards bear to live in our societies."

The original racial slur was "savage." But look closer at its meaning. Savage lives off the land. Savage has no pockets. Savage touches the earth with his feet. Savage doesn't mutilate the minds of his children. Savage reveres the shaman instead of medicating him. Savage runs. Savage hunts. Savage plants. Savage survives and thrives on his own accord. Savage is impervious to virtue because savage does not despise himself. Savage is any man impervious to Babylon's charm.

We are victims of our own Leviathan. The Civil War turned America into a puppet with strings. The final surrender at Appomattox only drove the Union Army north to focus on Indian removal from Ohio to Montana. Burning the South was necessary to break the land's knees. We remember the truth when we listen to the mounds. The American government was stolen not invented. The People of the Longhouse was a thriving bicameral government for 500 years. Canassatego suggested that the colonists form a similar nation and Ben Franklin advocated for its adoption.

"It would be a strange thing if six nations of ignorant savages should be capable of forming such a union, and yet it has subsisted for ages and appears indissolvable, and yet a like union should be impractical for 10 or a dozen English colonies." - Ben Franklin

George Washington visited the Iroquois Confederacy in council. He was infamous to the natives as Conotocarious, or "Town Destroyer." Washington's great-grandfather John Washington was called the "Devourer of villages." He called a parley with six tribal leaders and killed each of them when they arrived. The Mississippian culture was a thriving nation put down by the spirit of civilization. The mound city of Cahokia in Ohio had a population that rivaled London. Their roots were chopped down like the biblical groves of Asherah. Layer by layer, the bones of giants were sold off as the fragments and figments of dragons and dinosaurs. This land is your land only if you remember her. That is how speaking for the land works. We cannot speak for someone we do not remember.

CHAPTER TWO

Orange Man Sad

You find zeitgeist at the mall. You find truth at a flea market. The American mind is an appetite that's always hungry. "Epstein didn't kill himself" is a hotcake of law and order. Districts in Seattle and Minneapolis abandoned their city on purpose. Riots were funded with palettes of bricks placed on the streets. Barricades installed by city workers gave the liberated island of CHAZ its beach. The media pimped George Floyd's funeral with a golden casket. They called anyone who wasn't looting a racist. This is germ theory for the mind and the only cure on the shelf is more government. The double-headed eagle is Globalism and the New World Order. We jump from the mouth of one into the mandible of another. We are too engaged in survival to see the enemy's shape. Its wingspan is longer than the horizon.

The Epstein story brings conspiracy theories to the masses. "Trusting the plan" became a ticket into the truth movement. "Enjoy the show" is the lobby where Breitbart sells popcorn and PizzaGate. Trump could end this charade by walking down the stairs with the truth. But exposing the show would destroy America's delicate chandelier. Trump is catering to a billion points of light. Our hope for Washington makes truth a dying crone. Narratives must be salacious to be effective. What makes hope dangerous is how good it feels to carry it. We are fish in a barrel waiting for jumper cables. The dinosaur media dies peacefully while its new guard rushes in pretending to expose them. The letters of ABC, NBC, and CNN shriveled away years ago. The new media is nimble. It knows how to serialize a satanic tropical island cannibal temple into a pedophile reality show. If the numbers keep up, it will carry for two seasons. The new media is the old one in a fresh pair of sneakers. It's the stale salacious rumors from Weiner's laptop replaced by the fresh salacious rumors from Biden's laptop in an endless dangle of suspense from a chain. Despite every scandal they break, nothing keeps happening, over and over, again and again, forever infinitum.

We live in the land of holographic messiahs. Archetypes from the same factory roll off the assembly line gleaming in the sun. Geppetto is a spider spinning Epstein and Assange. It spins Hogg and Thunberg. It spins Pelosi and Newsom. It spins Clinton and Trump. These tentacles anchor themselves in the mind. Outrage is the sensation of its barb digging into the skin. Make 9/11 your litmus. Any media failing this test is unreliable. We are delusional to think 9/11 is over. There is nothing dead in our minds about it. There is nothing dead in our minds about school shootings. There is nothing dead in our minds about the Las Vegas gunman. There is nothing dead in our minds about Epstein. These events are cliffhangers by design. These are federally-sponsored clown operations designed to keep the system relevant and vital.

Trump wears orange makeup but no one seems to mind. Deep down, everyone knows this is white-collar wrestling. We look for politicians to play heroes and villains. We know it's a stage as we call them all jokers. But the joke hatched its eggs in our back a long time ago. We are bonding over the trauma of lying to ourselves. The Orange Julius Caesar is unrolling a New World Order to save you. Our vote is all he needs to keep us calm while it happens.

Voting is a suggestion box in a prison cafeteria. It's a gesture from the warden to those who find solace in hope. We are the children's children of Stockholm syndrome. Tulsi, Assange, and Trump all blame Saudi Arabia for 9/11. They sing in unison as the media harmonizes its two-party chorus. The attack on 9/11 required military and media compliance. No one has been fired, punished, or scorned. Those who know what's coming profit the most. America wrote the textbook for how to pillage a country. The poor steal televisions under the cover of a mob as the rich steal the rest under the cover of terrorism. The system works perfectly as long as people keep thinking it's legit. The alternative is too painful for them to swallow.

The moment we feel sovereign is the moment Babylon becomes irrelevant to our sovereignty. The more we take care of ourselves, the less we need government. To delegate responsibility is to abandon it. The land needs us to be its militia. We are its airspace, its wildlife, and its water quality. Washington DC can't even defend the Pentagon. The land needs men, not agency. Washington will continue to ravage its voters under the auspice of their protection. Real patriots would never trust their government. Trust is a flavor of obedience, and patriots are the antithesis of obedient.

"Enjoy the show…Trust the plan…Disinfo is necessary…Patriots are in control." - QAnon

Epstein saturation shows us how deep the cabal roots in the mind. Every lie is a virgin cast into the volcano and there is no one left but whores. Politics is the lion, the witch, and the wardrobe. A witch-burning always brings people together.

Roles like Hillary are crucial for politics to work. "They never thought she would lose" was the foundation of Trump's campaign. He was the Orange Outsider. The renegade champion waiting to pounce. He will get Hillary after he plays with her on the ropes. They said the same thing about Obama when he was the Lion. They said the same thing about Bush when he was the Witch. All of this drama is for the sake of drama. It's the only way politics can convince you taxes are real. How does "fixing" Washington DC prevent it from happening again in eight years? Voting is opium. It gives us all we need to lay there while the ceiling caves in. Revoke your consent from Babylon. Unregister to vote. Voting has always been the least you could do. To influence local issues, go to Town Council meetings. They are usually once a month and your witness is a powerful force in person. They will feel it more than your vote. Join the Planning Board or volunteer for a committee. This can be empowering and is more effective than voting. A vote delegates your responsibility to a stranger which is the same as abandoning it.

Calling it the Deep State is a form of denial. The government did nothing after the Finders Cult. They did nothing after Waco. They did nothing after PizzaGate. They did nothing after Anthony Weiner. They did nothing after Haster. What they do is publish child trafficking stories like WayFair. You troll the gullible with outrage. You dump chum in the water to sell shark repellent. Stop telling me elite human trafficking is real as we send our muzzled kids off to the mind factory on a yellow submarine. We tell each other we are deeply moved by the horror from the news because we know, deep down, none of it matters. Rumors garner more sympathy than our neighbors because rumors are horror sitcoms. The Lion is Trump. The Witch is Hillary. The wardrobe is whatever raises our nipples.

CHAPTER THREE

Propaganda Virus

A propaganda virus has struck home and masks are a symptom of its contagion. We are under constant attack from an electromagnetic frequency. There are two main sources of infection: the Associated Press (AP), founded in New York in the Spring of 1846; and Reuters, created five years later in London. No two organizations have done more to centralize and corrupt the world with a constant attack of information. Covid-19 shows us that countries are not what we think they are. Covid-19 shows us our weakness to propaganda from wires. If it required fuel to reach your ears, it is 100% propaganda.

All things come from belief. Science is prepubescent belief. Government is petrified belief. Wisdom is venerated belief. Everything we see is built on belief. On January 10, 2020, the first patient death attributed to Covid-19 emerged in Wuhan, China. The city's health commission reported patient zero had already been diagnosed with abdominal tumors and chronic liver disease. Despite the patient history, his passing was reported as proof of Covid-19. The entire world was suddenly on fire and no one had isolated the virus. A few weeks later, Italy reported its outbreak. Two months later, it was revealed as much as 80% of their tests were false positives. Hindsight is twenty-twenty, but the collective lacks a neck to turn its head around. By design, the propaganda virus went viral and the entire operation was fueled by taxpayer dollars.

On January 24, 2020, Donald Trump held a private meeting with top congressional leaders. The following day, Senators Loeffler (R), Burr (R), and Feinstein (D) began dumping a combined $11 million in stock just one week before the market's crash. The crash was blamed on the orchestrated pandemic for a virus that hasn't even been isolated. The media sang: "Even a negative test means nothing," "Millions must be tested," "We have to take these people out of their homes… even if they have almost no symptoms," "This is just the beginning." On March 5th, residents in Wuhan shouted from the windows of their homes, "Fake! Fake! Fake! Everything is fake!" as China's Vice Premier Sun Chunlan toured the new quarantine complex.

On May 15, 2020, the House passed a three trillion dollar aid bill adding to the Covid-19 bounty. Any hospital testing positive for coronavirus received $13,000 for every patient and $30,000 if they used a ventilator. Any president, any year, could say a virus is killing us and fund the statistics to prove it. This is the power of government. NASA fudged data to tell you sea-levels were rising in 2016. Eighteen intelligence agencies told you they found WMDs in Iraq. The 9/11 commission claimed Building 7 demolished itself due to fire. The National Science Foundation spends $8 billion a year to fund these beliefs and the people can't stop drinking its venom. Trump didn't invent the Covid-19 virus, he sold it. He sent every American a check for $1,200 as commission.

History is graffiti and the biggest paint can wins. What is happening on the ground versus how history will be recorded are as different as night and day. Paramedics aren't finding dead bodies from Covid-19. Hospitals are recording gunshot victims and automobile accidents as pandemic casualties. To date, one goat and one papaya have both tested positive for the virus. If more people understood this, they could see through the lie. But no one is paid to see through the virus – they are only paid to see it. Two lawyers argue a case. One side has $8 trillion to spend. The other has none. Who do you think will win?

"Denier" is the language of heresy. Scientism is a religion that lies to itself professionally. The good news is the virus is not dangerous. The bad news is the cure is designed to transform the world. The manufactured pandemic has been in the works since 1988. Its stimulus will end the petrodollar replacing it with a digital token. Centralized blockchain ends the ability for our children to barter privately or exercise free speech without repercussion. China's social credit system is already in effect in America. Trump's job is to let globalism get so bad we beg for a New World Order. The people who think everything is fine don't mind the government killing them softly. On Oct 18th, 2019, Johns Hopkins Center for Health Security ran a poll asking people how much information the government should hide from them. 50% voted Washington DC should manage the truth. Half of us are worried the state is coming for us. The other half fantasize how jackboots would be kinky. This is what the New World Order calls, "checkmate."

You can vote for any of the two candidates in a mask as long as you are wearing a mask. Nothing says "your voice matters" like voting in a muzzle. If anything shows you voting is bogus, it's Covid-19. Yet every corporation is deeply entrenched in the push for voter registration. This shows they work with the government to extract our consent. It shows us they are the same machine. Ghengis Khan did not kill his enemies, he seduced them. In 2019, over 1,600 CEOs stepped down making it the highest number ever recorded. These weren't punishments – it was compensation for cooperation. Every corporation backing the virus wanted this shutdown. Celebrities led the charge with Tom Hanks claiming the virus caught up to him in the outback of Australia. He was trapped in a hut with nothing more than a Corona typewriter and the trending column on Twitter. Everything is revealed in this apocalypse when you follow the red dot. The airplanes were never grounded which cemented the idea the pandemic was in every town. Overnight, it became vogue to catch Covid-19. Survivor stories bloomed on the AP and Reuters as dancing nurses in empty crash rooms became heroes. Ventilators flew off the assembly line to kill people behind curtains. Every CEO, politician, and celebrity knew the plan. Everybody's gotta get their shots and the market gets one to the head.

The International Monetary Fund reported 102 countries have been crippled by the response to Covid-19. America's corporations acting in unison have caused more damage than every recorded depression in history combined. The endless debt to every country continues to climb as the bull bleeds out on Wall Street. This is a one-world government and no one can make bail. On March 26th, 2020, President Trump offered a $15 million bounty for Venezuelan dictator Nicolas Maduro. The last independent nation was Venezuela and leaders like Libya's Gaddafi were the last of the Mohicans.

The difference between looting and pillaging is the tax bracket. Both take advantage of the environment. Both capitalize on a herd's feeding pattern. The biggest threat we face is electronic propaganda. Government and Hollywood have merged and it's trademarked by the Smith-Mundt Act. On Dec 21st, 1970, Elvis Presley got a DEA badge from Richard Nixon. The government has always worked closely with Hollywood. Fame is a matter of national security. People like Anderson Cooper and Sean Penn are embedded in the industry. In an interview, Penn told Cooper, "it's really time to give the military the full breadth and control of this operation." Penn declared, "There is no greater humanitarian force on the planet than the United States military." To date, our military has invaded thirty-six countries since World War II and not one of them has thanked us for our humanitarian force.

The only thing more dangerous than media are its addicts. The consumers of media work in hospitals and shape policy. They've long thought Trump was a Nazi but will side with him over anyone threatening media's legitimacy. Propaganda and fear are just that potent. News is spell-craft from a graphics department. The entire world can be shut down with words, and a single tongue controls them all. People who have called me intelligent and insightful insist I am irresponsible and heartless for doubting this virus. But humanity is not a virus and Covid-19 is an attack on humanity. With enough funding, everyone in America could test positive. What they are calling a test is a scarlet letter. These labels dehumanize mankind. This machine wants you in fear. It wants you to fear a virus. It wants you to fear China. It wants you to fear contact. It wants you to fear the public. It wants you to fear critical thinking. It wants you to love uniforms. It wants you to love procedure. It wants you to love celebrities. It wants you to love social distancing. It wants you to love 5G. It wants you to love Washington DC.

Credentials turn liars into fact technicians. Money is a powerful credential. In 1976, Rockefeller gave 45 million people a swine flu vaccination despite proof a pig virus can't live inside a human. It has to be developed in a lab to even survive the injection. Why did we develop a pig virus that could only be spread in a lab only to give it to humans? Better question, why did 45 million people agree? 2,500 people died within a few weeks of inoculation. Millions of survivors still carry pig material and mercury in their muscle today. Less than 10% of that mercury will ever show up filtered through the kidneys. An Army field medic calls metal lodged in the body shrapnel. The vaccine industry calls it herd immunity. The damages from the swine flu vaccine are still unknown. Spikes in cases of Alzheimer's and autism point to autoimmune deficiencies in tandem with vaccines. The only immunity vaccines contain is the one from legal prosecution.

We censor the word "retarded" to prevent us from talking about what vaccines do to our children. The last ones to admit vaccines are dangerous will be those whose job it was to give them. This truth is too painful to inject. A nationwide eugenics program was privatized on July 1, 1946, with the creation of the CDC. The Centers for Disease Control and Prevention dropped "prevention" from its title and no one batted an eye. The first wave was unveiled with the Cutter Incident in 1955 where 20,000 patients contracted Polio from the very first vaccine. The program went nationwide with the "swine flu" of 1976. If you are wondering who would do such a horrible thing, the answer is a human rancher. If you are wondering why humans need ranchers, I remind you 45 million people volunteered for the swine flu vaccine. Government is a necessity to the man who's lost autonomy. Babylon will always respond when we abandon our vigilance. The only reason we think voting is valid is because it's too painful to admit we pay a mafia to poison us with a tincture labeled, "safe and effective."

We don't even know what viruses are. We only have funding to develop vaccines to kill them. But viruses aren't even alive. Science can't even confirm germ theory. When we ingest toxins, bacteria form to do what our stomach could not. Bacteria surround the toxic waste to take one for the team. This is called the common cold. Pharmaceutical companies sell you petroleum syrup telling you your body is broken when it is working perfectly. When bacteria can't handle their job they become poisoned. Our cells react by secreting homemade soap. That soap is what we call a virus. Viruses are solvents that help the body. Viruses pick up the fallen corpses of bacteria on the battlefield. Viruses are combat veterans.

Medicine has long been a science of propaganda. The lie of Piltdown Man survived the scrutiny of science for forty years before an outsider exposed its fraud. We are decades, sometimes centuries, behind the truth. In 2011, Stefan Lanka won $100,000 in court for proving measles is not a virus. In 1884, German physician Robert Koch established a causative relationship between a microbe and a disease. He formulated four postulates used to show cholera and tuberculosis were caused by microbes. A budding industry falsely applied Koch's postulates to every disease and epidemiology was born. Eight decades later, In 1965, Koch's postulates were finally replaced with Bradford Hill's nine criteria for disease causality. Today, neither system adequately demonstrates a chain of contagion. Medicine is an ancient history of bottlenecking scrutiny for profit.

The only way you can be infected by a virus is through injection. That's the only way it works. Your body is a torus or a donut. It has an intake and an exhaust. The entire journey inside your torus remains 100% outside your body. The only way to put something in your body is through injection. This is the only way a foreign virus has a chance to survive. If you love your body, prove it. Tell your crew, right now. Speak into the intercom of your navel, "Attention. This is your Captain speaking. All viruses are awarded an honorary Morning Star. All bacteria have been given a Letter of Commendation."

Babylon is remodeling and germ theory is the blueprint.

The military is in the business of medicine. Ask yourself when did government become in charge of medical opinion. Ask how a second opinion is possible in a climate where seven trillion dollars is spent opposing it. Babylon's money is powerful stuff. It's a double-barrel snake charmer in the religion of science and medicine. Even after insisting Trump was Hitler, they wanted him to round people up and rape them with needles.

America is a pyramid economy and CEOs were its keystones. Trump removed each of them one-by-one. The right to assemble has fallen somewhere between a felony and a misdemeanor. Private property has become mythology and children are biological wards of the state. The pathogen exists in our misplaced trust. Our weakness comes from denying the predator of Washington. He declares war on humanity and Trump buys 1.8 million face masks to cover it up. The only way to fight this contagion is with humanity. The only way to save civilization is to stop wearing a muzzle. Seven million people died during the Great Depression. The Surgeon General said this would be our 9/11 and Pearl Harbor moment. History will only remember these headlines. History will only remember the tents waiting for the bodies. History already believes in the virus even if we do not.

The truth of vaccines has already come to light but the vaccinated have been turned into vampires. There is no coming back from thinking your life depends on a needle. Biting everyone around you is the only way to stay alive. The vaccinated don't want you to feel better – they want themselves to feel better. It takes electricity to admit they were at fault. It takes even more to push back against a system's credentials. Even when those credentials are used to do harm. The people who administer vaccines are victims. They joined the system to help people and that system lied to them. They cannot admit the system is wrong. They can only hide behind its marketing language. Abortion is reproductive services. Genital mutilation is sanitation. Fentanyl is medicine. Mercury is safe. Aluminum is effective. Radiation is therapy. Ignoring diet is practicing medicine.

Even climate change is fueled by germ theory. It claims humanity is a germ poisoning its environment when man is the environment. Man is 100% natural. Everything he makes and does is natural. Man is not a problem. Anthropogenic germ theory is the problem. Modern medicine has built its entire foundation on germ theory. Germ theory is the idea that the poison comes from the inside. Terrain theory is the idea that the poison comes from the outside. Hospitals can't consider terrain theory or diet because the patient has been isolated from their terrain. This is the practice of protocol, not medicine. The system was rigged long before its practitioners got here. Dawn Lester and David Parker in their book, "The Real Science of Germs," prove germ theory is flawed in two sentences. You can have a specific germ in your body and not be sick. You can be sick and not have the specific germ. There are 380 trillion viruses in the human body. Germ theory will declare war on every one of them.

CHAPTER FOUR

New World Normal

The world is in quarantine. Parks and streams are off-limits to the public. Turns out these resources never belonged to us. They were privileges of Babylon. Stores installed plexiglass cages to hide their muzzled employees behind see-through walls. The public is a dangerous animal. The world is a salad bar and everything gets a sneeze-guard. The stupidity is so loud that no one can listen to reason. You can't quarantine someone who isn't sick. That is, by definition, impossible. This is a consent virus. Most of us have no immunity. The credit card machine is covered in a plastic bag. The hunchback clerk mumbles at me to slide my fingers inside where everyone's hands were magically sanitary. Shelves are empty except for wine and beer. Cold, fermented resurrection is always ripe for the picking.

A nurse friend scolded me for not taking the virus seriously. I asked him to educate me about what he was seeing on the front lines but he could not. I cannot find a single provider willing to share any horror stories about Covid-19. Despite the rumors of carnage, twerks on TikTok from nurses with plenty of time to practice their choreography are trending every day. Hundreds of reports have come in from empty hospitals. Video after video of empty crash rooms surrounded by multi-million dollar equipment. Why? Only a few doctors and nurses have the electricity to ask that question. The only thing harder than convincing a soldier they are committing murder is convincing a nurse they are committing homicide.

In a foxhole, there is no procedure to stop a war. On a battleship, there is no procedure to stop a torpedo. In a Covid-19 pandemic, there is no procedure to stop a ventilator. It is estimated that 35-80% of patients died from a government-mandated procedure. A procedure that made the hospital $30,000 per patient. The only thing that can save people is humanity. But every patient that dies makes it harder for the machine to change course. Changing course means it was wrong and the system can't be wrong. There is no difference between nurses and soldiers. Both are trapped inside a procedure. We see it manifested in their uniforms. We have to stop calling these victims heroes. We must call them human. Upgrade them so they can find the strength to break out of their procedures and think.

Covid-19 credited deaths will continue until everyone submits to medical martial law. Only then will the numbers decline for good behavior. This is the New Normal Order. If you disagree, your neighbors look at you as a biological terrorist. If you work in medicine, you are a new elite class of essential worker. You covet the special permission and papers needed to travel. This feeds the narcissism of those who are already emptied. We are living in a reality of privilege where everyone is tainted. Not by sin, but by blood. Everyone has tested positive for the humanity virus.

Everyone behind the mask is pretending the government never lied to them. This is why in the future, you won't be able to drive a car without a vaccine. Certain businesses won't let you in, "Out of respect for those with vulnerable immune systems." The new racism will be called immunism. The healthy will be considered a new kind of "white privilege." Society will continue to reward the "sick." Hollywood will raise them up on a pedestal. The LGBTQ flag will add another stripe to the top of its seating chart. If you take the vaccine, you will exchange your humanity for a special credential. Everyone wearing a mask is participating in the procedure. In two generations, everyone will be either vaccine compliant or living outside the gates of Babylon. The body's immune system is the final frontier. Whoever controls that market will become a living god. They will hold the keys to every human's immune response and only the richest can get it back.

Politicians aren't what we think they are. Viruses aren't what we think they are. Vaccines aren't what we think they are. Countries aren't what we think they are. Schools aren't what we think they are. Birth certificates aren't what we think they are. Government is not what you think it is. Borders are not what we think they are. Only animals may cross a country's border without a credential. Humans have no such freedom. What we call government is a filter we use to swallow the truth. Countries were invented to hide humanity's fence behind a colorful bush. We've been living in FEMA camps this whole time. We only call them countries to play along.

Here's what we know. On April 2nd, jobless numbers doubled in a week from 3.3 million to 6.6 million. There are mandatory mask-wearing laws across counties in every state. Facial recognition cameras work best when everyone is six feet apart. Artificial intelligence can count masks to gauge who's compliant with the propaganda. Walmart has installed cattle lines. Food rationing is in full effect. Every Town Hall is closed. Every church is closed. By April 15, 2020, over six trillion dollars in cash has been liquidated with much more that's still too hard to count. Trump unrolls a nationwide 5G building emergency. Indian Reservations have their federal trusts revoked. The DAPL permit has been revoked. The Presidential Seal went missing on March 14, 2020. There was no Presidential Seal on the podium for an entire month of Trump's press conferences including, March 19th, 20th, 22nd, and finally on April 10, 2020.

The worst thing that could happen was normalcy and its venom settled into our back. The hunger game ends round one and everyone gets a fifteen-minute break. The world will be sedated with cash while the virus sets in. The Covid-19 lie is memorialized in every obituary. Regardless of precondition, it's a badge of honor for the hospital and a community to proclaim, "We suffered, too." Heart disease, cancer, and strokes are all down thanks to Covid-19. How can we know we're not the virus? This question will be squelched by the slow drip of novocaine. Our reptile brain will decide the New World Normal is not a concern. It drops its guard to save calories. It's going to need them in the future.

We are living will. We are the trinity of reptile, mammal, and man. We are three strings plunked, hammered, and muted. These are the days of lizard kings. Our spine is crowned in an ivory tower. Our neocortex has been sodomized for so long, it gave up completely. It wears bunny ears now like a grown-up Macaulay Culkin asking for rape. The victimized mind must choose between sadism or masochism. Everything is inverted but we've learned to enjoy it. We skate backward like teenage girls drifting in circles around the rink. The only one who makes sense is the town pariah. He tells you the truth you don't want to hear. The 9/11 spell of two towers is now the spell of 19,495 new 5G towers distributed nationwide as a matter of national security. Trump mentioned the importance of securing these towers from terrorism. Trump has declared Antifa and the KKK domestic terrorist organizations. If you don't see what's coming, you might be wearing rabbit ears, too.

For the next several months, Trump will mend his relationship. He'll tell the economy he never meant to hit her. He'll tell us how much he loves her in whispers of, "America First." He'll tell us all to pick out some jewelry with a check in the mail. The entire world is finally in the pocket of the hidden hand. No one needs to force anyone into a cage. If anything, people need forcing out of one. It's like the Jim Jones cult except instead of drinking Kool-Aid people are injecting each other with aluminum.

They are erecting an invisible fence in broad daylight while no one complains. Perhaps, I am simply jaded. I see a killer on the road and want us to do more than blink. Many will throw tomatoes, but this truth is ultra-violet: the lawyers, nurses, and doctors have failed us in this plan-demic. They abandoned their post as watchmen to serve the machine. They executed their orders perfectly without question. They left vigilance at home in the freezer during a crisis never realizing crisis is always the weather when they loot us for liberty. Maybe we'll figure this out the quadrillionth time around.

My call to arms to all lawyers was met with nothing. The Minutemen are in meetings and their voicemail is full. All of them stake a claim in the corporate fiction. They are the Dukes of Acronym. They insist letters own property and sue free men on the letter's behalf. How does one trespass against something without a body? These illusions are run by boards. These boards are made of wood. That same wood is the puppet elected to regulate them. Everything they show us is imaginary voodoo, drizzled in white paste. We are children eating glue. All we do is grow taller and longer with age.

The land can never be ruled. Only our mind is vulnerable

to that fiction. Underneath the concrete is the truth. People wearing ties scroll by it like neanderthals frozen in the ice. Their eyes are open but none of them can speak. How could they? Lawyers know the truth but have been trained to survive. Pro bono pats them on the back while we sink in quicksand. We are lizards paying taxes by chopping off our tails. If you think Republicans are going to save you, you're a Democrat. If you're a Democrat, you're not even reading this. So how much more, before we consider, maybe possibly, making an appointment to become suspicious?

None of us are alone. It just feels that way because we live in houses. Border checkpoints inside your country mean it's not your country. The towers are going up. The economy is coming down. Vaccines are pushing in. The moat is filling with water. Every border is surrounding us and we are plugging ourselves into its walls. Celebrities are drinking to our hunger game. They ran the toilet paper shortage story to joke about how we shit our pants. Ladies and gentlemen, the predator is in the trees. There is no such thing as government. There is no such thing as country. There is only Washington DC.

We are the soil underneath the concrete. Our future is crystals, silver, bullets, and seeds. We are the tribe who hunts metallic panthers. Our spines are precisely as tall as we think they should be. Our aim is true. Our gut is right. We are amperage held back by shame. We are electricity insulated by propaganda. We are plasma shorted by doubt. Deep breath. We will find each other under the moon.

Each of us is a campfire waiting. Tune into the land as a protector. Listen to the trees. The Sun card in tarot is the Corona (XIX). This is a magic of nineteen. This number is the amplifier behind Covid-19. This is the 19th anniversary of 9/11. Pull all your consent back into your chest right now. All it takes is the oscillation from your vocal cords to revoke that contract:

"I do not believe in these people who call themselves the government. I take all belief and consent I have given them and place it upon my shoulders. They have proven themselves unworthy of my lifeforce and belief."

I declare war on the people who make war on things. Human ranchers have been weaponizing panic since the devil and the witch. It evolved into Hottentots, the Indians, the Nazis, the Japs, the Commies, and the Arabs. When that stopped working, it was the mafia, the nukes, the acid rain, the asteroids, and the WMDs. When that failed it was sexism, racism, toxic masculinity, and immigration. When that failed, it was time for Covid-19. If you eat a cheeseburger you test positive for Covid-19. These are the tricks and tools of government. Panic is the business of the machine. Anyone applying for the job empties themselves to its luxury. Men fall on the battlefield bleeding ink all over their contract. Their dead bodies are left walking the streets, smiling blankly. The pay is great. The seats are great. The wine is great. The parking is great. But the song remains the same unless we rip the speakers from the trees. If we don't, they will keep playing this tune, over and over, until all of us sing.

On March 27th, BlackRock was authorized by the Feds to save the economy using Chinese assets. America and Chinese economies have been merging under the ocean since Rockefeller. It makes zero sense for Trump to call this a "Chinese Virus" unless he wants to stage a war. This is exactly like the feuds on camera in professional wrestling. The expression, "behold, a pale horse," didn't always mean death and apocalypse. The Indians called the pale horse high noon on their medicine wheel. A pale horse was the bright, white sun of truth. The truth is: these people have been planning an apocalypse for a long time now. They knew the Great Awakening was coming. They turned it into a controlled demolition. Just like they did with the two towers, nineteen years ago, in September. Only truth stops this music. It wasn't 19 boxcutters. It wasn't Covid-19. It was the 19th anniversary of 9/11.

Only by knowing what's happening can we turn this energy into something positive. There is a powerful plasma behind belief and consent. Humanity must lose its trust in a government shepherd. Our authority is abandoned by its delegation. The fix is to place your consent back in the land. Place yourself deep in her soil and choose her over it.

CHAPTER FIVE

Gifts of Baal

Lies show us truth. Abortion teaches us sanctity. Vaccines teach us discernment. Psychopathy teaches us empathy. Circumcision teaches us blindness. Delegation teaches us abandonment. Foolishness teaches us wisdom. These are the gifts of Baal. They are too painful for many to open. But if we do not accept them, Baal keeps laying more at our feet. Nothing else can teach us like Baal can. This is why Baal is here. Baal is as brutal as he is effective. Best we open his gifts quickly.

A shrinking violet withers to secrete my sympathy. I cry my pollen of spores so the bees will come to take it away. Spring is the heart burning its way into summer. May the fall rise so the hungry can partake of this rapture. The frog teaches the scorpion as much as the scorpion teaches the frog. Nothing dilates a man like a woman. The woman is my jungle. She is my apex predator. There is no other opponent more formidable than her. Heartbreak is a gift of Baal. Fifty-five percent of all marriages end in divorce. Perhaps this is their purpose. Marriage cracks a man open like nothing else can. We consider pain failure but pain is the opening of a husk. It's the tearing away of a gift's wrapping paper.

War is a gift of Baal and America is its chief recipient. Every 1.3 years, we invade or bomb a sovereign nation. Every four years, we vote for someone to put the military on steroids. The United States is teaching its people how blind they can be. We plant land mines for freedom. We drone strike schools for peace. We set oil fields on fire to protect their sovereignty. War is a gift that's hard to open so Baal keeps bringing us more. In 64 countries around the world, there are 110 million land-mines still lodged in the ground. In 2020, the Pentagon has over 3 million anti-personnel mines in its arsenal. The "Toe-Popper" and the "Bouncing Betty" are still alive in Cambodia. Every month, six people are killed or injured. Since 1975, over 40,000 Vietnamese have died by the hands of our taxes. America has attacked thirty countries since World War II. Many on more than one occasion. Baal's gift teaches us it is wrong to fund violence. Baal teaches us it is right to defund Washington DC.

Politics is a gift of Baal that shows us we are fools. There are only two candidates. There are only two parties. Why do we believe white-collar wrestling is real? Why do we think the most expensive and powerful military ever assembled is left under the control of one of two people and no one has been able to corrupt the process? The military budget is $1 trillion per year. The Republican and Democrat party budgets combined are less than 1% of that figure. Any vote is consenting to more violence. We are participating in psychopathy by sending more money. This gift of Baal will keep on coming until we stop.

NASA's Apollo hoax is a gift of Baal that teaches us the power of cosmology. We see them spend $56 million a day to manipulate our belief. We accept NASA because it gives people what they crave. Privacy. Atheism is the quest for privacy from God made possible by God's gift of amnesia.

We create the vacuum of space to stop our voice from reaching God's ear. We create a Big Bang to stop our sight from reaching his eye. Scientism is the veil we use to hide. The path to finding God begins when we decide he is missing. NASA is gifting humanity something they desperately need – spirituality.

Satellites are a gift of Baal. Satellites are high-altitude balloons maintaining elevation higher than civilians are allowed to fly. The 1947 Roswell Crash was a high-altitude sateloon. The local newspaper got it right. The military seized on the crash to reinforce the idea of a space program. The official Roswell press conference was a government-staged propaganda operation. On the fifty year anniversary of the very first UFO sighting recorded in a newspaper, The Air Force came out and said they would no longer investigate UFOs. Air Force Colonel John Haynes told the press pool he had promised a mysterious man a question in the back. A voice hidden from camera asked if the Air Force would release certain evidence. Haynes made it clear the Air Force would never speak on the subject again. This press conference came at the height of popularity for the Fox television show X-Files and made the perfect cover-up cliffhanger. The military is the media and the media is the military. News is the fondue of propaganda and science fiction is its dipping sauce. All of these operations are clown operations from the CIA. We are watching them spend our consent tokens on a lavish wardrobe for the public's fantasy. Space is a circus of lies and the U-2 spy plane is its ten-million-dollar clown car. The high-altitude CIA runs the satellite program from these planes. The U-2 program has shaped foreign policy. It led to the building of the Berlin Wall. Today's Lockheed U-2 spy planes don't need a pilot and don't need to land. Each of them is a flying computer farm equipped with plug-and-play "satellite" modules like telescopes, cameras, dish broadcasting, weather imaging, radar imaging, and more. Google is showcasing this technology to the public with their high-altitude broadband service right now. Our belief in space is a gift of Baal that won't stop giving.

Secrecy is a gift of Baal. Vannevar Bush founded the Manhattan Project, the National Science Foundation, and the weapons manufacturing company Raytheon. No one has done more to bring the atomic bomb and nuclear weapons to the international table. The Manhattan Project employed 130,000 people and 130,000 of them had no idea what they were doing or building. This international program was a joint effort of the United Kingdom, Canada, and America and the idea came from a 1914 HG Wells book, "The World Set Free." Physicist Leó Szilárd read the book in 1932 and conceived the idea of a neutron chain reaction and filed for a patent in 1934. Compartmentalization mixed with the love of fiction is a gift that teaches us the danger of blind trust.

Countries are a gift of Baal. We fall for the illusion of flags like we fall for the illusion of football teams. But the colors tell us more than we are willing to digest. In the Book of Revelation, the colors of the Four Horseman of the Apocalypse are the state colors of Afghanistan, Egypt, Iraq, Jordan, Kuwait, Libya, Palestine, Sudan, Syria, UAE, and Yemen. All of their flags were designed in 1916 by a British Diplomat, Mark Sykes. Sykes was a key negotiator of the Balfour Declaration and a supporter of Zionism. The Balfour Declaration was a hundred-year-long plan responsible for creating the modern state of Israel and the eradication of Palestine. Additionally, the flags of Finland, France, Indonesia, Netherlands, Poland, Thailand are offshoots of Norway's flag. The flag of Switzerland is the Templar Cross, the world's oldest and wealthiest international subterranean society. It's the same Red Cross seen on medics and the only symbol sacred on all sides of every battlefield. When we believe all of our countries as competing with each other it becomes easy to fool us with Sputnik. The first space race with Russia was the beginning of many races using fantasy technology from the pages of science fiction. Countries have never been what we thought they were. They are subterraneanly controlled for their owners' safety and insurance. Borders are seating sections in the same colosseum built by an international mafia a long, long time ago.

Sanctity is a gift of Baal. Many times, "I will pray for you" can mean "I will prey for you." It takes a broken spirit to use prayer as an energy weapon. If people were sincere, they would simply pray for you. They could tell you about it after it happened, not before. I ask the ones who promise, "What time are you going to pray for me? Will you text me when you've delivered?" Redemption becomes an energy game when everyone is cursed to the pit. Telling someone to repent is how you unpray for someone. All of this can escalate quickly into, "My Christ will beat up your Christ."

Scientism is a gift of Baal because atheists will believe anything. Covid-19 is a living god and science worships the Baal Corona. Masks are his vestments. Economies are his sacrifices. PCR tests are his scripture. Seven trillion dollars is in his offering plate. Dancing nurses are his acolytes. Doctors are his deacons. Fauci is his Pope. People who don't believe in the Baal Corona are his heretics.

Wikipedia is the Bible of Scientism. It's got the Creation Story of Evolution, The Bill of Ten Commandments, The Saints of Mount Rushmore, The Cities of Hiroshima and Nagasaki, The Pilgrimage to the Moon, The Sermon by the Crook, The Crucifixion of JFK, and the 19 Boxcutters of 9/11. Even scientism's mantras are gifts of Baal: "I believe in science" or "I trust science." Both of these are the antithesis of how science is supposed to work.

California is a gift of Baal because Californians have always agreed to their government. The spell over that state is so blatant it's camouflage. From taxes, regulations, environmental shaming, neglect, theft, and corruption, California is not an accident. It's a living 9/11 we pretend is just bad luck. California lost by trusting its government. It remained loyal despite the poor forest management, massive taxes, penalties, environmental policies, equality warfare, needle programs, poop maps, sodomy parades, communism, fascism, nepotism and a ton of pornography. Baalifornia is a gift of Baal that is burning through its package.

9/11 was a gift of Baal. We learn the media can sell us anything. We learn the news never claimed it was true. We learn the twin towers could have been empty. Tenants in the towers was told their lease was up and to move out before the demolition. That would explain why a building that accepts 200,000 visitors a day with desk space for 50,000 workers only had 2,996 casualties. The Port Authority, NYPD, and NYFD are so bloated and corrupt they were left in the dark by pure bureaucratic incompetence. Many are still dying today from mesothelioma after attempting to rescue bodies from a planned demolition site. Bureaucracy is a blindness that's hard to fathom if you've never been chewed up by the machine. It will keep happening until we accept its gift of Baal.

CHAPTER SIX

Mask Psychosis

I had to place a mask up to my face to hug my mom yesterday. No way am I not hugging my mom. No one forced me. I could have refused, but I'm not a psychopath. At least not yet. I was a black sheep long before Covid-19. The corona simply makes everyone's coloring more obvious. I only reach my family on a superficial level now. And that's only when I participate in Babylon. We can share its topics and trends which I haven't embraced since high school. It's as if we were at the family table talking to each other through a mask. My mom trusts Oprah more than me. My dad trusts Fox News more than both of us. The good news is I finally understand none of us need to trust to love each other. Love is gravity and we are here in a circle around a fire. It's just more superficial now. Family is a quantum entanglement. Like trees talking to each other through the soil, I know they are here. I love my family. It is a big fire. But despite the fire, I haven't really seen them since I was twelve. At least not on a deep level. Babylon separates us all with its dissonance. We've always been hiding behind some kind of mask to survive it. The apocalypse has made it easy to see.

This world is suffering from mask psychosis. I've been stressed about this global reset virus for a while now. But having to cover my face to hug my mom is the deepest cut to date. Babylon is brutally nice and polite. It's safe and effective and it's only as hard as wearing a mask to hug your mom, buy food, earn a living, or move in public. If you are in Babylon, none of these things are a problem. If you are out of Babylon, these things destroy the core of who you are. This core is meaningless to the people behind the mask. They can't value something they've never had.

Sometimes, it seems our mission in life is to be punished by people we love for lacking the ability to read their feelings. I embrace this mission now. It is truly my gift of Baal. It allows me to hone my empathy to levels I would never go on my own. The people you love most are your dojo. Love makes them a brutal opponent to overcome. You can't destroy them. You survive with them.

In Babylon, the definition of a good person is one who doesn't question the mask. Doesn't question the virus. Doesn't question the quarantine. Doesn't question the government. Doesn't question the politics. Doesn't question the media. Doesn't question the 5G. Doesn't question the schools. Doesn't question period. The same people who believed nineteen boxcutters took out the most sophisticated military in the world believe masks will save us but only if everyone wears one. But if masks are so important, why take them off at home? Isn't a family's safety worth a little discomfort? Aren't we saying families aren't as important as strangers in public? If we're going to play this charade why not take it all the way instead of doing it superficially? People see right through this but they pretend anyway. That's what makes it so brutal. It's why so many feel comfortable hiding their face. They are ashamed of how easy they fell for it all. Except at home. At home, we're reasonable about how stupid all of this is. Wearing masks is retarded. This is so retarded, society had to put a stigma on the word retarded to try and stave off how retarded we could be.

A human cannot communicate behind a mask. Only words can pass its prison at visiting hours. I peel my ears to imagine someone's face as they talk. I point to their mask and shake my head saying, "I can't understand you." My statement is polyphonic but only his brain is listening. There is no somatic information transmitted through a mask. We are built for facial recognition. It's our brain's primary function. Masks turn us into walking text messages. Medical professionals wanting me to have 72 shots of aluminum say if I was injured they would treat me as if it was doing me a favor. They justify abortion, circumcision, vaccines, masks, germ theory, and social distancing under the blessings of procedure. Sleeping men in white coats hunt children from allopathic tree stands and we call them pediatricians. Their credentials are so heavy it overrides their conscience and sense of morality. These are the same credentials used to experiment on animals. They've been told science comes with diplomatic immunity.

Before one is moral, one is amoral. Before one is holy, one is aholy. Masks are fashion and fashion is mind control. Fashion changes our prana economy with others. A single mask creates a gate for shame to flow. This gate requires a polarity to open the circuit. The masked is one pole. The maskless is its opposite. When they meet, a gate is opened. Masks are detrimental to our energetic immune system. How one feels is contagious and we've created a nationwide witch-hunt for a virus we can't see. Stop being nice about masks. Nice is cover for being dishonest. Children are watching. Show them we won't tolerate dissonance. All of us are strong enough to manage this apocalypse. We fail by hiding what must be revealed.

Today's rebel is mask-less. Remind people who think they

are on the frontlines of Covid-19 that Marines thought they were on the front lines of saving Iraq. This isn't a new game. It's the same game over and over but many are too ashamed to stop playing it. We are breeding two kinds of people in the alchemy of Covid-19. The first kind believes in masks, politicians, germ theory, media, racism, sexism, xenophobia, and everything they were ever told in school. The second kind of people don't. This is the difference between exoteric and esoteric. Exoteric seeks for truth without. Esoteric finds truth within. This apocalypse is a division between blind dogma and discernment.

Thank you for not wearing a muzzle. You are holding humanity above water. Imagine how hard it is to be a child trying to read someone's face or a deaf person trying to navigate a world surrounded by masks. A viral video of an elderly man at a shopping complex in Wales told the cameras why he no longer wanted to live, "I only came here to see the smiles. It was all I had to live for." Man is buried with his convictions. All of us must choose wisely.

CHAPTER SEVEN

Victim in the Hood

You know it's all bullshit because no one goes around bunking things. Yes, bunking. We don't even have a word for the act of verifying someone's propaganda. We only have a word when we debunk it. We live in a world where everything is true until someone spends the fuel to prove it false. A system like this does not deserve our energy. The $21 trillion lost during 9/11 was never our money. To call it ours is a first-class seat to victimhood. The truth is we gave that money to them. All of us did, every year, with our taxes. No one needed a gun to take it from us. We gave it to a mafia for their protection. They promised not to take even more of it by force.

We lie for the profit of calling ourselves victims. We are the piston of Kronos and his steel bit rests in our mouth. Our leathery reigns are wrapped around his saddle nonchalantly. None of us want to leave his side. Victimhood is bliss. It charges its owner with the feeling of innocence. To be persecuted by evil is to profit from it. The victim bonds with their savior and persecutor to complete their energy triangle. To climb out of victimhood is to end a painful addiction to energy. This is an expensive process that will require a lot of calories so buckle up.

Victimhood is a sail we harness. Victimhood is a conservation of energy. There's a reason hope came from Pandora's box. Hope is the cherry on top of victimhood. It feels counterintuitive, but all movement sprouts from resignation. Hope is a kind of holding on. But man needs to give up. Man is a motor who fails his way to resiliency. Failure only happens when we learn to let go. Death itself is a great awakening. When we surrender, we shed hope and all the fear that comes with it. We stop lying to ourselves to feel good. Abandoning hope feels bad because we fear hope's liberation. But hope stops us from passing through the portal into the unknown. Hope is its own salve. It only cures people who were feeling hopeless.

The opposite of hope is courage. Courage is a man who thinks he is worth more than his condition. Hope keeps us sinking. Courage keeps us rising. Hope and courage are opposite poles. Hope is not good for you. Hope is good for victims. No one is doing this to us. They are selling us the way to do it to ourselves. Once we see victimhood as something we need, the veil is lifted. Are we truly enslaved or are we simply afraid to rise?

Allow me to rape your victimhood. The psychopaths didn't put you to sleep. Your DNA is awakening from dormancy. It must be illuminated to reach its potential. Until it does, we are collectively afraid of waking up. We chose to give our consent to programs that help us shed power. This is the slavery of medicine, cosmology, psychology, and politics. We short ourselves out in all these realms so we can remain on the floor. We crawl to avoid the fear of standing. This truth is too shameful to admit so we don't. It turns out we are the psychopaths keeping ourselves down.

There are so many different varieties of victimhood. Each is a strategy aimed at offloading the practitioner's power. Victimhood is a practice one does to oneself. It's a sleight-of-hand trick we use to avoid ownership. And it's everywhere. It's built into the wallpaper. The Devil has always been victimhood in drag but we curse anyone who tries to expose him. God casting us out of the garden is victimhood. If we are rejected by God we can now meet his low expectations. Suffering in silence is a form of underground victimhood. We extract guilt behind someone's back and charge them interest as they don't pay. It's a nasty prana economy. We expect more from people and feel victimized when they disappoint us. It's massively twisted how clever we can be at victimhood.

Being a victim of evil doesn't make us good. Being a victim helps us but we are too embarrassed to admit it. Being a victim helps us believe we are good because victims are supposed to be innocent. But we are not innocent. We manufacture and distribute morality 24/7. We produce good and evil every day of our life. We are so much more than good – we are real. Real is deadly and dangerous. Real is alive and we fear the responsibility outside our hypotheticals. We cling to the safety of calling ourselves good or calling someone else evil. Both of these statements make us feel the exact same way. Victimhood is electrically profitable to our psyche. It saves us calories. That's why it's so hard to stop. The body is stocked with a pharmacy of chemicals willing to lie for our benefit.

Like all rabbit holes, the way out is up not down. Many are still convinced the people that lied to them left a key at the bottom. Like any lottery ticket, all they have to do is trust the plan and keep scratching. The more time they invest in a story the more they need it to be true. Need is the addiction to victimhood. To need something is to want its fix. This is the slang of drug addiction. Victimhood needs perpetrators. Victimhood needs winners and losers. Victimhood needs to be saved. The key to overcoming victimhood is putting yourself back in your body and cranking up the engines. We find all our power once we conquer our fear of the responsibility.

If you want to discover your victimhood be nice to it. We can't spot victimhood when we keep so much shame packed around it. Realize victimhood is an electrical gate in our system. We open it to offload power. We close it when we have shed enough to feel comfortable. Hunt victimhood in your language when you hear the pronoun, "they." "They are doing this to us…" "They are trying to…" "They want us all in…" "They" is an airlock we use to abandon our warp core. As we offload power through these gates, we also gain power through our collectors. Our spine is the largest collector. Claiming energy is as simple as claiming responsibility for ourselves. We monitor the gauges of our language, feelings, breathing, and posture and learn where we leak power. The less power we leak, the more we get to practice holding.

CHAPTER EIGHT

The Lorax of Men

Man is the Gulliver of his travels. He ties his feet together to complain about his predicament. I grow angry at his silence. I clench my fist at the thought of him doing nothing. Again and again, man mocks my serenity with his apathy. He is worse than cruel. He thinks nothing of doing nothing. I poke his living corpse like a dead snake in the road. Again and again. Over and over. All he does is nothing. All man ever does for himself is nothing.

Yesterday, a masked man confronted me on my mountain at the local general store. He scolded me for my naked face as he wagged his finger. I disagreed with his tort but he insisted, "You must not be from around here." He was wrong about that and I told him. He insinuated I was contagious and ordered me to step back. I would not. I sunk my roots and tore into him like a jelly sandwich. The young clerk looked like a guilty raccoon too afraid to pick sides. The man was older than me but shorter by several inches. His hands were shaking as he reached out for his receipt like a life-rope. His lungs were grasping at straws as he fumbled a signature he'd written thousands of times before. He shook his head to console himself. I spoke for the land and he knew it. There would be no mask ordinance. The man took his groceries and hobbled away on his wobbly knees. After my purchase, I saw him outside in his car fumbling its automatic transmission. Behind an N95 mask, inside the climate-controlled window of a luxury sedan, he flipped me a middle finger and sped off. His indictment was a ping-pong against my brick wall.

Find your center. Make it contagious. If the mountains make you happy, you must make the mountains happy, too. The land does not speak to you, it speaks through you. You are its living soil. You are its fingers, voice, and morality. Unity is not your strength. Self-supremacy is your strength. Self-supremacy scares the crap out of people who worship media and government. Supremacy comes from experience, not regurgitation. Experience is the only truth you know.

Your true state is a verb. It was a birth certificate that got you thinking like a noun. That was your first credential that laminated itself to the outer shell of your ego. It capitalized, assimilated, and incorporated you into a person and crowned you with the thorns of a citizen. You sign that contract every moment with your belief. When we believe ourselves into a sheet of paper, we are frozen in its words. Words enroll us in language and trap us in their labyrinth. Language treats us like property which makes us feel wanted. We feel meaningful and important inside words. They can also enslave us in the binding of a contract. We are haunted and enchanted by the belief and comfort we derive from our credentials. We go to school for credentials. We go to work for credentials. We lock our kids inside a classroom for credentials. We punish them for daydreaming by blemishing their credentials. We reward their obedience by decorating them.

"And that no man might buy or sell, save he that had the mark, or

the name of the beast, or the number of his name. Here is wisdom. Let him that hath understanding count the number of the beast: for it is the number of a man; and his number is 666." - Revelation 11:17-18

All of your credentials are sealed to the mark or the name of the beast. Your name in capital letters is the "name of the beast." Your social security number is the "number of his name." Having "the mark" binds the blood to a name making the name superfluous. The mark links all of our contracts and credentials to your genetic line. To shame our mark, our name, or our number is to release its energy for trade on the open market. Many can feel the flow of cold electricity when they read about the "mark of the beast" in Revelation. Belief is enrollment. It gives a circuit energy. A real loss of prana is felt when we degrade humanity into a beast. Beasts have credentials. Their contracts are traded on the market. If you believed you were worthless, your mark would sell for cheap. If you knew you were priceless you could not be bought or sold.

The land needs men. Too many have sold themselves to the machine after it convinced them they lacked the credentials for judgment. Do not worry if you are on a government watchlist – insist on it. Speak like your ancestors are listening. Penalize people who want to believe in news. Make it expensive for them to keep watching. News never tells you its stories are true. There is no disclaimer in the opening or closing credits. Its truth is an assumption we make based on the costume and pace of the broadcast.

I am the Lorax of Man. My only government is the solstice. She is my savior and my resurrection. She dictates my seasons and my shadows. She gives me the light of her judgment every day. I am a tribe of one. My nation is indivisible. I give the land nineteen stomps to tell her the giants are home. I am one of nineteen. There are more of us coming. Every new moon a campfire beats the land's heart. We give the land our witness. It was always hers. Our bones are her stones and our arteries are her branches. We are the branders of aether telling her story to the constellations to bask over.

CHAPTER NINE

Eye of Ra

Many researchers have stumbled across the Black Eye Club. This unofficial club is a collection of photographs from leaders in every industry each with the same black eye. Everyone in the club has a publicist. Everyone in the club wears makeup as part of their job. These people have committees to decide how and when they should be seen in public, yet they all seem to be showcasing a black eye with no explanation. Pope Francis had a black eye (Left). So did Pope Benedict (Right) and Richard Branson (L). George Bush (L) had one, too. John McCain (L), John Kerry (L), Joe Biden (L), Prince Phillip (R), Prince Charles (L), Prince Andrew (R), Tony Blair (R), Charlie Rose (L), and even Harry Reid (L) all had black eyes photographed in public. And these are just the politicians. David Bowie (R), Kayne West (L), Anderson Cooper (R), and Tom Hanks (L) had one, too. Hank's photo even came with a napkin bearing the caption, "I am not allowed to talk."

Rumors of secret Illuminati fight clubs are hardly a satisfying explanation. Other reasons for the black eye include surgical procedures to the face, such as a facelift, jaw surgery, or nose surgery. These men certainly aren't getting facelifts and many of these politically embarrassing procedures could be easily hidden with makeup. It would seem, these black eyes are meant to be seen. They are a sign of initiation. Before we speculate on the purpose for this club, we need to understand the Eye of Ra.

People think the right brain is creative and the left brain is analytical. But that's only true for right-handed people. A person's dominant hand is wired to the function assigned to each lobe. A left-handed person has a dominant right brain which means the right lobe handles most of the language, memory recall, and math. Their left brain is specialized for simulation and creative procedures that acquire estimates and guessing. Both sides of the brain work in tandem on just about every problem it solves. The brain is two towers and man discerns truth between its poles.

Awareness is a singularity. All of life must come to us through its gate. Consider the anatomy of your nervous system. Everything you perceive is a binary signal of action potentials at 100 millivolts. These electric telegrams are a Morse code of sodium and potassium. A rapid series of exchanges is a loud signal. A slow exchange is a quiet one. Regardless of the signal's volume, the transmitting voltage remains the same. Only their frequency is different. Every dimension of nerve sensation uses this binary protocol. None of these signals come with timestamps.

Without a timestamp, the thalamus has no way of knowing its origin time or how long it took the impulse to travel. This presents an impossible task for signal interpretation. Signals from the toes take longer to get to the brain than signals from the fingers. As the body grows, so too does the distance a signal has to travel. Sounds move slower than light in the retinas. Smells are localized and don't even route through the thalamus. All of these problems tell us we are missing a mechanism to collate and sort their order for the brain. In engineering, this would be solved by a central processor.

How does your body know which signals come first? We know the pineal gland generates a circadian rhythm to monitor our sleep. We know there are localized circadian clocks found in other places of the body like the retinas. But these chemical cycles lack the fidelity to synch the entire system accurately. This problem is solved if every sensation we had first came through a central point of origin. This zero point is the pineal gland or the third eye. But as we are about to see, it is more accurately our first eye – the Eye of Ra.

One day Shiva's wife Parvati, playfully placed her hands over his eyes. Suddenly darkness engulfed the whole world and all beings trembled in great fear as the lord of the universe had closed his eyes. Suddenly a massive eye of flame erupted from the forehead of Shiva; a third eye had appeared there and this gave light to the world.

The world comes unfiltered through the Eye of Ra. This gland is a single point in the center of our skull. The pineal gland rests on the keel of two lobes. This is our mercy seat between the wings of the cherubim. Your skull's temple is Solomon's Temple. Inside its holy place, the Eye of Ra keeps our covenant with God. We have a Sol, or Soul – a personal Sun. We are the fiery eye that sees all. But what we see and what our senses reveal are not the same. We only sense what our instruments can handle. Our senses are built for comfort. Consciousness needs an aperture to limit the flow of reality. The pineal is the eye into a world of fire. Its light would burn our retinas to behold directly. Instead, we are fitted with a unique lens, or aperture. We control the diameter of this opening to control the amount of information that flows through. Light is color and information. A larger aperture allows a deeper spectrum in light's intelligence to flow through. Your senses render more information.

The retina's rods and cones give our vision gender. There is a sexual polarity in our retinas. Macular vision is the obelisk. We use it to focus on a specific spot like a laser. Peripheral vision is the reflecting pool absorbing everything around it. Most of our endorphins are tied to what we see. Our eyes are Pavlovian drool balls turned inside out. They are smugglers of light's rumor. Aperture and intelligence are not the same. Aperture is about one's ability to accept more reality. Intelligence is about one's ability to reason what the aperture has presented.

Blindsight is proof for the Eye of Ra. Blindsight is the ability to respond to visual stimuli without the eyes. This should be impossible without the use of the retina's rods and cones. But multiple experiments prove blindsight is real. This ability comes in two flavors: spatial and emotional. Perception signals can be triggered in the amygdala despite the subject having no sight. Even more profound is that emotional triggers can be perceived from nothing more than a photograph. People see their environment without using their eyes.

In an earlier experiment, one of the authors of the new paper, Dr. Alan Pegna of Geneva University Hospitals, found that the same African doctor had emotional blindsight. When presented with images of fearful faces, he cringed subconsciously in the same way that almost everyone does, even though he could not consciously see the faces. The subcortical, primitive visual system registers not only solid objects but also strong social signals. [https:// www.nytimes.com/2008/12/23/health/23blin.html]

Tracing the anatomy of the eye we find the retinas routed through the amygdala and into the occipital lobe. It is in the amygdala that we see a link to the pineal gland. We have had our understanding of sight backward. It is the Eye of Ra that perceives the world uninhibited. It routes this signal into all of our perceptual dimensions. Sounds are routed to the ears. Colors are routed to the eyes. This singularity to the amygdala allows the body to filter the signal and throttle it down to a comfortable level. This throttling is what makes our aperture. All of our vision and hearing are constricted from the amygdala using melanin and dopamine. Just as truth is suppressed by society to make it comfortable, so too is information suppressed by our amygdala to protect its pilot. Aperture is a lensing of consciousness. Like a muscle, the aperture dilates as our system becomes comfortable with perceiving more reality. Ignorance isn't just bliss. It is the key to survival.

The retinas are always working. Even when the eyes are closed. Even while we sleep. The eye's hardware suffers burnout requiring a rebuild every ten days. Nothing burns out faster than our rods and cones. The retina's gallery is opened by the flow of dopamine. Mice are completely blind without dopamine. Dopamine tunes a retina to a factor of 10 billion and render anything from a sunny day to a moonless night.

The retina employs melanin to absorb light. Melanin blots out the information coming in through the rods and cones. Like the brim of a hat, melanin helps us see better when the sun is too bright. Dopamine and melanin are the gas and brake of the retinas. The same mechanism for throttling reality exists inside the ears. The ears have dopamine which is vital for operation and the inner ear produces melanin which modern science can't explain why.

Speaking of eyes, our skin is covered in pores. Humans, monkeys, apes, and horses have a unique sweat gland physiology. Unlike other animals, our skin is covered in sweat glands that produce melanin. Melanin does more than give skin its color. We see the world through our pores. You feel them working when you get goosebumps. All people have roughly the same number of melanocytes; the more melanin made, the darker the skin. Exposure to sunlight increases the production of melanin, which is why people get suntanned or freckled. The more light piercing in, the more melanin lowers the visor.

Aperture is the lensing of consciousness. Aperture is not synonymous with success in society. Subjects with higher aperture perception are often demonized, drugged, and diagnosed as mentally ill. We lock them away so they won't make the rest of society uncomfortable. But the term "reality" is a majority opinion. The true nature of perception is multiplex as none of us can see the whole picture. We only fathom what our body is equipped to absorb. Without the amygdala, our system would melt, our speakers would clip, our hearts would burst from too much signal. We would freeze like a possum from the weight of the headlights coming at us in the road.

So much is being discovered about consciousness by studying patients with schizophrenia. What the industry calls audible hallucinations have been known to be shared by multiple people. Jerry Marzinsky documented thousands of cases while working with incarcerated patients. His decades of work in the field, show a ramping of signal as patients seemed to open their aperture. The auditory sensations would come first. These "voices" would grow into shadows that would appear in the room. As their aperture dilated more, the shadows developed eyes that would glow. Many visions were shared by multiple witnesses which prove they weren't hallucinations. Their aperture is seeing a reality others cannot. Associations between schizophrenia and ocular misalignments are documented including strabismus (cross-eyed), and it's opposite exotropia. We see the same abilities of aperture dilation in shamans. Dr. Malidoma Patrice Somé explains a shaman is someone who has learned to be comfortable with seeing their whole environment. What western medicine labels mental illness signals the opening of aperture in his country. "With schizophrenia, there is a special receptivity to a flow of images and information, which cannot be controlled," stated Dr. Somé. "When this kind of rush occurs at a time that is not personally chosen, and particularly when it comes with images that are scary and contradictory, the person goes into a frenzy."

Aperture is crucial for sensation. The body is tuned to perceive a whisper but the true volume of reality can be a roaring lion. The entire rainbow of radiation observable to the human eye is only a tiny portion of the electromagnetic spectrum – or about 0.0035 percent. Dr. Somé sees a lot of "beings" lurking around his patients that are invisible to other people. In Africa, these patients would be encouraged, not drugged, as emerging healers.

The biggest proof of aperture comes when we study albinism. Albinism prevents the body's melanocytes from producing melanin. This problem is compounded because the body doesn't have a way of detecting whether or not melanin was successfully produced. The amygdala signals the melanin but the melanin does not respond so the eyes and ears see a world unbridled. The Coexistence of Oculocutaneous Albinism with Schizophrenia is a published phenomenon. [https://www.ncbi.nlm.nih.gov/pmc/articles/PMC7008756/]

It is not a coincidence Noah was an albino. His appearance was described in the Dead Sea Scrolls, "the flesh of which was white as snow, and red as a rose; the hair of whose head was white like wool." Jesus could be one, too, when we read Revelation 1:14-16, "The hairs of his head were white, like white wool, like snow. His eyes were like a flame of fire." We know Jesus was a necromancer. The Book of Mark showcases his talents at removing demons. Jesus, Noah, and others could have seen these demons thanks to a dilated aperture. We know the word messiah comes from the Hebrew word Moshiach which means anointed one. We have archeological evidence of trace cannabis found on temple altars. The Messiah, or anointed one, was someone who's aperture was dilated with ritual, endocannabinoids, and dopamine stimulation.

PTSD suggests trauma rips the aperture open. Soldiers become addicted to guns. Ambulance drivers become addicted to adrenalin. Fighter pilots become addicted to speed. Rasputin's life and writings seem to confirm the theory that pain dilates the aperture. So too do the rituals of John the Baptist, Odin, Sundance, and even the Crucifixion. Man values dilation more than happiness. When we are dilated, we are fully alive. Even sadism and masochism point to man's fetish for dilation.

The Eye of Ra is the origin of perception. The pineal sees all by sensing the environment's perturbations. Perturbations are reality's totality vibrating around us. The pineal sees a multi-dimensional raw feed of source unfiltered. This primordial source penetrates walls, time, physics, light, and sound. Everything you experience through your senses come from this primordial source. We reduce it into the tangible dimensions like sight and sound.

Source begins in the Eye of Ra's sandbox. From the pineal, it is filtered through the amygdala and occipital lobe before being sent down Plato's cave, the optic nerve, and into the retina chamber. Inside, our reality is seen as shadows painted on the walls of a cave. This cave is the retina wall. Our eyes and ears are seeing the shadows of flickering torches lit by a roaring sun beaming through the pineal.

So Jacob called the name of the place Peniel, saying, "For I have seen God face to face, and yet my life has been delivered." - Genesis 32:30

Phenomenon like voices, aliens, demons, ghosts, ball lightning, targeted individuals, and Sasquatch are how an aperture renders energy. People with a larger aperture see more energy. Our amygdala places this energy behind a veil suitable for consumption. People say you can't trust your senses, but if we did not trust our senses they would show us everything with devastating consequences. You can think of mainstream media as an aperture. You can think of atheism as an aperture. You can think of fear or compassion as an aperture. There are many ways to see source through a pinhole.

The eyes and ears are galleries, not windows. Our crystal ship is listening to the future inside our temple. It sees what our eyes are about to render. This means there is an unknown delay from source to sense. This delay can explain phenomenon like deja vu. The Black Eye Club could be an optical procedure to remove the limits imposed by melanin and dopamine. The Eye of Ra would show patients a raw feed of reality through a gallery that's unable to dress it in a costume.

CHAPTER TEN

White Lies Matter

Lies are the abyss of gnosis. Lies are the taffy holding this matrix together. Lies are truth's incubator. Lies are important. Lies are necessary. Lies cast us out of the garden. Lies give us privacy. Lies give us identity. We are naked without lies. We feel shame when our lie is exposed. Genitals are called privates because they are a secret. This secret is the core of who we are. Lies are not monsters. Lies are the only thing keeping us from falling apart. Lies give us security when we need it most. Lies give us fashion. Lies grant us nourishment. Lies win us survival. The more we understand the purpose of lies, the easier to admit when we make them. We lie every second of every minute of every hour of every day and it's the only way we will learn truth.

There is no commandment in the Bible against lying. At least not completely. We suffer breach for bearing false witness to another but this commandment doesn't include lying to oneself. It is peculiar God would fail to tell Moses the evils of lying. It could have replaced either of the first two commandments with plenty of room. Instead, the Lord knew man needed to lie to himself. Lies are important to keep reality malleable. We need lies to render the missing pieces of our world. Lies form the primary fabric of reality. They allow our aperture the flexibility to dismiss what we see right in front of us.

People can't admit they lie because they believe themselves to be good, and good people don't tell lies. This is a lie we tell ourselves which is God's way of being funny about good and evil. People are neither good nor evil. People are real. People are so real they lie. Even so real they lie about lying. If no one lied, no one would discern. If no one discerned, no one would know truth. We are surrounded by lies because we need them to forge truth. Our ability to see lies in government is a new sensation for most of us. This information is painful to look at and we needed time for our aperture to adjust to the pain.

The moment we notice a lie, we join its quest for truth. Every truther enrolls in a secret society without knowing it. All of us are masons at the base of a pyramid building a lodge of truth. We chisel holes in the foundation's propaganda as we carve away its keystones. We are following God's blueprint with our eyes closed. God teaches those who learn and fails those who do not.

There are some among us who have already mastered God's truth. They know it so well they are teaching the rest of us with lies of their own. You could call them liars and you'd be right. You could claim they're evil but you'd be wrong. In March of 2020, two white ships decorated with bright red crosses surrounded the land of the plumed serpent. The USNS Mercy (T-AH-19) harbored in Los Angeles. The USNS Comfort (T-AH-20) docked in New York City. The ritual of two towers was stretched across America from coast to coast. These ships are the masonic pillars of Boaz (mercy) and Jachin (comfort). The same two towers that rang on 9/11. The American Red Cross is an ancient symbol of the Knights Templar. Even today their ensign is considered sacred in war.

The symbol has been charged for centuries by the world's most powerful magicians. These magicians consider lies a necessary instrument in the Great Work. Realizing the world is made of lies is painful. Understanding why is liberating.

Deceit is a type of current. If you believed nuclear weapons were a threat, you'd be open to someone stopping them. If you believed chemtrails were a threat, you'd be open to someone stopping them. If you believed child sacrifice was a threat, you'd be open to someone stopping it. All of these share the same blueprint of mind control. None of these need to be true for the mind control to work. I'm not claiming any are true or false. I am claiming it doesn't matter for their circuitry to work.

Deception acts like a capacitor to store and release the power in a truth. People who have affairs are stealing electricity. The deceit drains the victim and feeds the perpetrator. This is why so many love triangles are so profitable. Cheaters say they are "confused" or "searching" or "misunderstood" but they're harvesting someone's energy to create passion. If you are having an affair you are a polygamist. The least you could do was be honest about it. But that would take away from all the free electricity. People having affairs don't love each other as much as they love electricity.

Potlatch is the art of giving for the sake of giving. We spoil potlatch by revealing its source. When the donor avoids the credit it keeps the potlatch pure. A special kind of deceit is employed when making potlatch anonymous. We seal its identity in a lie by omission. There is real power in lies. Lies are secrets. To hide the truth from everyone is to own it. To cover it with a lie is to hoard it like gold. Lies are how we secure power by keeping the truth hostage. Lies are how we protect our bounty from thieves. Lies are as constructive as they are destructive. They are the grease of free will providing each of us the ability to believe something unique within a multi-player environment.

Consciousness is the aperture of a camera. The larger the opening, the more light comes through. The sting of lies opens our aperture like a lotus. Lies cause pain which dilates us enough to want truth. Lies pollenate us to bloom. Lies are built into humanity's language and thinking. Friends lie to make each other feel good. Parents lie to their children about Santa Claus, the Easter Bunny, and the Tooth Fairy. Mass consciousness lies to its people about vaccines, germ theory, and war. The hidden hand of God grooms its children with the power of lies. It is wrong to think this means God is cruel. The truth is too soft a comb. Lies are perfect for pulling through the tangles. Our aversion to the comb hides the love and care that went into its tugging.

Not all love is evidential. There are five levels of love and humanity can only experience four of them.

Five aspects of love:
1. To love as child
2. To love as partner
3. To love as parent
4. To love as stranger
5. To love as God

To love as a child is to love as slave. We love our master for what he provides us. Our love is congruent with our survival. We love because we survive. The first level of love is the most convenient and profitable to understand.

The second level of love is to love as an equal. Siblings, friends, and partners know this kind of love. This love is reciprocated and conditional. This love is two-sided and mutually beneficial. This kind of love is easy to grasp once a child grows up to be an adult.

To love as a parent is to love as master. We love our children despite their dependencies. We love them so much, we need nothing in return. A child may rebel and a parent will still love. This kind of love is a one-way sacrifice that can never be noticed or repaid.

To love humanity is to love as stranger. One can love the community and express it through charity. This kind of love plants trees for people you will never know. This kind of love is beyond intimate. This love requires no witness to validate or return.

To love as God is to love simultaneously in all directions. This kind of love is completely ineffable. God loves everything as it is. God loves the broken as much as the fixed. God loves the falling as much as the rise. God loves every aspect, corner, and shade of the world. God embraces the shadow. God nurtures the darkness. God completes the fractal.

CHAPTER ELEVEN

Dojo Earth

Welcome to Dojo Earth. You painted your world with such stunning resolution you fell into the canvas and forgot. Well done. You may not remember why you came. Don't fret, that's all part of the amnesia. You asked to come here. You wanted to learn, but God could not be your teacher. You would call him cruel every time he knocked you off your feet. You would have no one to run home to when the lesson was over. God chose someone he trusts to be your teacher. His students call him Sensei. His victims call him Satan.

God did not cast you out of the garden. This was a lie you told yourself and you feel its shame when you are naked. You came to Dojo Earth to be transmuted from lead to gold. You opened the door and amnesia hit you in the face. This is all part of Dojo Earth's training. Your memory has been blindfolded. You are here to find your way home in the dark. God sees you through the window. God will never disrespect you or your training by coming on to the mat to correct you. This would make Dojo Earth useless. God trusts sensei. You do not trust sensei because sensei smacks you in the face with a board. It hurts so much we curl up into a ball. We wail on the floor for hours about how unfair it was to catch us off guard. The comfort of being victimized keeps us on the floor. Victims feel persecuted to numb a deeper fear of being vulnerable. Dojo Earth is here to remove the vulnerabilities that cripple our authenticity.

Dojo Earth is the idea our home is not broken. All of the lies and dissonance you see are a vital part of your training. Everything is working perfectly. The vitriol is what you came for. Dojo Earth is a terrarium for consciousness. Each of us has a unique aperture to bloom. The dojo wears many costumes and uses many techniques to train you. Sensei demands you take every lesson seriously. He will push your limits every day and demand more and more of your authenticity. The dojo teaches you how to stay buckled in your cockpit. Stay centered and you will thrive inside Dojo Earth. Look at the students who came before you. You are trained by the teacher of Attis, Buddha, Dionysus, Hercules, Horus, Jesus, Krishna, Mithras, Osiris, Tammuz, and Zoroaster. You are wasting time taking the dojo's punches personally. Sensei stands over you laughing to make whining expensive. You struggle to see how sensei could be helping, but sensei knows how to get you back on your feet. Sensei wants you better than you are. Sensei wants you taller in your spine. Sensei works for God, not you.

Dojo Earth is an arena armed with every kind of deception. We are tumbled like rocks until smooth. People wake up thanks to the psychopathy. Psychopaths have been doing us a favor. They're giving us something our parents never could. They are teaching us vigilance. Blind trust is a water that must be broken so we may take our first breath. Inside Dojo Earth, there is no evil. There is only a lack of compassion. Compassion is not consent or agreement. Compassion is an instrument of emotional telepathy. When you exercise your compassion, evil dissolves and all that remains is understanding. We need this weapon to meet our opponent on the mat. When we understand what motivates them, we witness their weakness and our opponent disappears.

These questions prove we live in Dojo Earth.
1) Why show Building 7?
2) Why fake school shootings?
3) Why spare the Challenger Shuttle crew?
4) Why ask for our consent?
5) Why show Corona at the Olympics?
6) Why warn of the fire at Notre Dame?
7) Why isn't mankind already in chains?

There are students of Dojo Earth here to help. The Building 7 reveal on 9/11 was a sacrifice of power to awaken a thousand points of light. You are one of these filaments. The Covid-19 reveal in the opening ceremony of the 2012 Olympic Games was done for the same reason. The Notre Dame fire was revealed 33 days earlier when the movie I Pet Goat 2 was released. These were all part of the Great Awakening. This is the purpose of America as a shining city on the hill. Columbia is Prometheus unchained. The Statue of Liberty's feet are unshackled. She is the bright morning star and a symbol for a nation of philosopher kings.

Mankind's illumination is the Great Work. The Illuminati participate in this alchemical process. They believe they are doing God's work by trolling you into enlightenment. These people have understood this world for a long time because they had a jumpstart on history. America was built by the Illuminati to participate in God's plan. They don't do this for our sake. They don't do this for mankind's praise, or to hear themselves called humanitarians. They do this for God's witness. They believe God sees them helping. The Hopi call the Illuminati the Tribe of the Rainbow People. The prophecy says they have come to move consciousness into the 5th hoop. All people will join the Illuminati once they have been illuminated. What hides us from truth is the thought we don't deserve it. The corona is here to make this hiding impossible.

The deeper the lie cuts, the more we crave its truth. This would be a good strategy for bringing a world together. Lie to everyone about everything so much and so bad everyone stops what they're doing to demand the truth. It turns out dissonance is how you get someone to live in tune. This is the only way you can be sure to spark a universal motivation. It's painfully accurate that relentlessly brutal and repetitive lies make a man value truth. Nothing else will do. We know a New World Order is possible because truth would be the one thing that could bring everyone together. Not every elite has to be evacuated or evil. The only thing that could truly unite the world into some kind of New World Order would be truth. If they wanted a slave camp of mindless drones they could have that already. Something grander is planned. Look around. Vitriol is everywhere and its results keep leading more people to truth. People are waking up faster thanks to the alternative being offered. The lies are helping. The more salacious the better. They went so far as to name George Floyd's elementary school teacher, Waynel Sexton. Let that name sink in by saying it out loud. Her name was Waynel Sexton. Maybe these clowns are lying to you in hopes you will stop believing them. If you were the Illuminati and wanted people to stop believing the media, Waynel Sexton would be something you might do.

Bill Gates could not be a bigger household villain, yet he has done more to push for vaccine truth than the entire antivax community combined. Gates has been pictured with books that were ripe with conspiracy theory fodder like, "How to Lie with Statistics" and a children's book about poisoning everyone in the world. He's on camera describing the act of "shoving a needle into a child's vein and squeezing the plunger. " Note, vaccines go in the muscle, not the vein. The over-the-top salaciousness of Bill Gates can be explained as an Illuminati troll. Gates has sacrificed his entire life's reputation to play the villain of vaccines. He will forever be demonized in public yet he was sinisterly waking people up to vaccines the whole time. Bill Gates will never be credited by the population for doing this. His sacrifice is hidden behind the mask of Kali. This makes it a very special kind of potlatch to God.

There are no forms to sign to join the Illuminati. You don't have to eat a baby or choke a white rooster. This is a free-range tribe running clown operations all over the world. They compete with real predators for control of your mind. So many more of us would be slaves if they weren't helping. You may even thank them eventually. You might even stand up and lend them a hand when you realize its the lies that make people bloom. All of those calories are making it the Best Apocalypse Ever.

[FADE IN]

PUPIL: "Good people would never lie."

SENSEI: "Good people want you to discern."

PUPIL: "Good people would never ridicule my misfortune."

SENSEI: "Good people want victimhood to be expensive."

PUPIL: "Good people would teach me gently."

SENSEI: "Good people did and you fell asleep."

PUPIL: "You are Satan!"

SENSEI: "I am Sensei."

PUPIL: "God will punish you for this!"

SENSEI: "God told me to do this."

CHAPTER TWELVE

For the Love of Vitriol

Take heart, for we have already died. We are only here to write our eulogy. In alchemy, V.I.T.R.I.O.L. is the latin acronym for "Visita Interiora Terrae Rectificando Invenies Occultum Lapidem." It means "Visit the interior of the earth, and by rectifying you will find the hidden stone." Vitriol is a formula for perfection hiding inside an ugly word for strife. Modern society hates vitriol. Ideas that scare us the most are packed with electricity. They require a sacrifice of fear to unlock them.

Man's ribs can be either a cage or a cathedral. It all depends on how he frames his heart. God throws vitriol into our capacitor to see how well we hold its charge. He is testing us for integrity. These are opportunities to prove ourselves hearty. We are grateful for the chance to hold more witness. We welcome the vitriol of this apocalypse with open arms.

The year 2020 will mark the 19th anniversary of 9/11. The vitriol you have been feeling came from an alchemically controlled demolition. Building 7 was an initiation into a hermetic order. Your quest for truth is your climb up Jacob's ladder. There is no going back. That bite was a pilgrimage to the golden dawn. Chew it up and swallow. Don't rest on the floor as its victim. The more vitriol pushes, the farther it takes us. The matrix runs on strife and we ride it like a slipstream. Smell the plasma of dawn through the nose of a vulture. It dines on the carcass of resurrection. Breathe in the dawn and smoke it like a reefer. Implore your enemy to try and stomp you. Vitriol is the thermal we need to rise.

Man blossoms in vitriol. He bleeds salt from his sweat and tears. His thorns are a crown that he earns. A man blooms in scorn. His chest is a nest that's been tested. Man is alive when he bleeds. Woman is alive when she nurtures. In Rhinebeck, there was a gathering of nineteen. The moon rode the back of Jupiter. Birchbark was gathered nearby for parchment. People wrote spells to purge in the flames. Each member approached the fire respectfully and gave it their secret. I wrote nothing on my bark. I stepped forward and planted both my feet as I gathered the tribe's witness. I held the moment to show each of them I claimed their time. Their silence was a handshake to our agreement. It takes a certain amount of electricity to hold a tribe in silence. I made my exchange of calories and cast my intention from my throat, "Vitriol." I called in the gods of strife and offered them the chance to refine me. I was there to seek, not release. The alchemy was instant. The next day, one of the tribe was shouting at me on the porch. Since the ceremony, I have lost many of those friends around the fire. I called in alchemy's lightning and it was delivered on several occasions. We are sharpened by our tribe. We face each other on the mat and the winner is the one with the most authenticity.

Let truth carve her fingernails into my back. I pour myself like an ocean into that which is empty. I am Poseiden and nothing can stop my wave. I am a hunter of those who forgot. I ping them with my empathy till they remember who they are. I am the King of Dolphins. I have always had a fetish for sharks. We mine the deepest vitriol in love. The only thing worse than an addiction is never having one. Each of us is born with a fetish for human touch. If we're going to spiral, we might as well do it like a Fibonacci. To love the spoon that carves out the heart is to love the art of cooking. We are seasoned in salt and oil. We feed ourselves to each other in bite-size pieces. We dine on each other's hearts like Aztecs on a pyramid. We stick our fingers in each other to see if we are done. We are endlessly cooked in passion's fruit and flame. She says to me, "I must abandon you." I ask her why. She said, "Because of how poorly you handle abandonment."

CHAPTER THIRTEEN

The Six Belts

We abandon ourselves by insisting we are good. As evil is done in the name of good, so too is good done in the name of evil. The road to heaven or hell can be paved with each other's intentions. Your opponent is anyone in the dojo who brings you vitriol. Vitriol is raw material you can alchemize for your growth. It is your authenticity on the mat that determines how well you do against your opponent. Your mission is not to defeat them. They are here to witness your authenticity. Their witness is the prize you seek.

Your job is not to change your opponent's mind. You are here to manage your prana economy. What your heart repels you make expensive. What your heart embraces you make affordable. Our authenticity is forged and honed under vitriol. Our opponents are vital for this growth. We bow to them with respect for the gift they bring. This is the only way to accept them. None of us are wise alone. To see wisdom in others is to make room for it in ourselves. Recognizing an opponent's wisdom carries the same epiphany as mining it. Compassion is a tool. It allows you to look deeper behind your opponent's field to gain advantage.

The more energy we collect in our capacitor, the more energy we have. Your opponent will adopt a position and stance congruent with the amount of power they have at their disposal. This power will determine their strategy. Knowing the strategy helps you meet your opponent on the mat. Your opponent's strategy is never wrong. It is directly tied to the amount of heart power, or ego, they have available.

There are six belts:
    White Belt - Power of Trust.
    Yellow Belt - Power of Fear.
    Red Belt - Power of Rage.
    Green Belt - Power of Compassion.
    Blue Belt - Power of Commandment.
    Black Belt - Power of Resurrection.

The White Belt is a strategy for an opponent who has no power. The white belt is armed with ignorance. The white belt has no ego or pride. He fears no enemy because he does not believe they exist. The white belt does not have enough energy to use his discernment. He will swallow narratives and regurgitate them like trivia. The white belt has no power to lose. He lacks the capacity to hold it. He can't afford the calories it takes to be afraid.

The Yellow Belt is fear. It is the first step above white. A yellow belt has enough power to generate fear. Fear is caloric. It requires fuel which is expensive. A yellow belt's fear is his source of power. It gives him just enough energy to rise from his knees to his feet. He lacks the electricity and capacity to think of anything beyond his survival. He will gather fear from his environment to keep his field full.

The Red Belt is anger. It is a step above yellow. It requires more power to generate anger than fear. The red belt sees the predator everywhere. A red belt's anger is his power. It gives him the energy required to move. He lacks the electricity to think of anything else but the enemy. He will gather anger from his environment to keep his batteries full.

The Green Belt is compassion. It is a step above red. It requires more power to generate compassion than anger. Green belt sees the predator bleeding. Green belt has enough heart power, or ego, to empathize. Empathy can be a powerful weapon. It shows the green belt where his opponent is weak. He sees his opponent's motivation and use it to his advantage.

The Blue Belt is commandment. It is a step above green. It requires more power to generate commandments than compassion. The blue belt motivates his opponent with authenticity. His voice is powered by his empathy and his ability to speak the truth. The blue belt can turn multiple opponents into allies with his voice.

The Black Belt has the aperture of Jesus. They witness a reality that is fully dilated with the power of necromancy and personification. The black belt holds the power of resurrection. They survive and persist through every persecution. These students need intense vitriol to continue the work of refining their core. The ghettos and slums are the ideal home for these alchemists.

If your opponent gains more power than they are comfortable handling, they will shed that power instantly. They will create a prana economy with any opponent they can find, anyway they can. Most of the time, this shedding is done with victimhood. Victimhood is how the neocortex justifies the electrical system offloading its power. Its reasons are pointless. All that matters is what's happening to your electricity underneath. Victimhood flows differently for every belt.

White Belt - Victimhood of ignorance

Yellow Belt - Victimhood of fear
Red Belt - Victimhood of anger
Green Belt - Victimhood of compassion

Someone with anger issues punches a wall. He has too much electricity and needs to remove it instantly. The amount of violence and pain he causes is directly proportional to the amount of power he feels ashamed and afraid to hold. Now he is victim to the pain he inflicted on himself and can begin to drain his excess power.

Someone with fear issues gets nervous in front of crowds. Their field takes on too much attention and they can't hold that power. They leak it through stuttering, stumbling, or forgetting their lines. The goal is to lower their stature in everyone's eyes. If everyone witnessing them were to lower their expectations, the victim would feel better with less power running through their veins. Or so they think.

The white belt is victimized by his addiction to ignorance. They believe all news by default. They call anything else a conspiracy. They insist it must be true or it would not be the official story. The sheep rarely has to shed power because he so rarely finds any down on his knees.

Even the green belt sheds power by violating their own boundaries and practicing codependency. They castrate themselves as empaths or the victims of narcissists. They create a scenario for others to violate their boundaries so they can offload energy to the victimhood of trusting someone who hurt them.

Every belt uses victimhood creatively to offload excess power. Learn to recognize it in your stance. Once you do, you will see it in your opponent and can use it to advantage.

CHAPTER FOURTEEN

Chariots of Fire

We are chariots of fire hiding behind sheepskin. We run from our reflection through the forest. Underneath our hair shirt is a coat of many colors and we are tired of reducing things to coincidence. You'd think synchronicity would bring us comfort but there is too much shame in being naked. Shame must bloom before it blossoms. A woman is beautiful when she is naked. She extracts man's salt before he comes. The salt of man is sand in her hourglass. Every grain is a testament to his attention. We cannot pause God's witness till Sunday morning in a church. Every second of every day is a holy communion with someone.

The District of Columbia is a masonic ladder for humanity to climb. But the hardest woman to love is Lady Liberty. We cast sin between her legs and curse her for bringing the dawn. No one can sleep with her light on. We are farmers refusing to plant seed until God comes down and drops one in every hole.

Venus is Isis, the Holy Virgin. We chopped off her fingers and hair in the grove. We cast her naked body into the pits of Rome. We erased her name from every scripture. We crucified her in the sky as humvees hunt her down in the desert. Ritual arson bursts open her hymen at Notre Dame. Its black smoke pulled on the wailing forgotten bones stacked along the miles of limestone catacombs underneath Paris. Man makes a whore of Babalon's virgin and renames her Babylon. She is raped to be made pure.

We are the soil between Satan's salt and Lucifer's oil. We are defiled by one and liberated by the other. Time is a lamp burning in the holy place and the ego tends its altar. The heart is a vortex of aether endlessly conglomerating. We stand our ground between two criminals. We are portable, pulsing, perturbating, humanoid suns. We are circuits of God's electricity. Open your eyes to the morning light. The sun cannot burn that which is made from itself. He is El Dios del Cobre, the Copper God. You are staring down the barrel of his living connection. You are his signal and his instrument.

"I, Jesus, have sent my angel to give you this testimony for the churches. I am the Root and the Offspring of David, and the bright Morning Star." – Revelation 22:16

The Greeks called Venus the noctifer at sunset. At sunrise, she is called the lucifer. Lucifer and noctifer were aspects, or phases, of Venus. The meaning of Lucifer was bastardized by King James, the same man who tortured herbalists in the name of witch-hunting. It was King James who first personified Lucifer by turning it into a proper name. There are Native American ceremonies like the Sundance that incorporate the morning star. Odin, Jesus, and Osiris are all referenced as dawnbringer or the morning star in their literature.

The fear of Lucifer is directly proportional to man's fear of his own potential. This is how archetypes are wired. We say Prometheus stole fire because we fear illumination. It ruins the fun of hiding in the closet. We don't like seeing ourselves stuffed behind the coats down on our knees. Many of us are not ready to hold the torch. We hide from it behind the fear of God's punishment. We use God like a child shielding himself behind the legs of his mother. Prometheus was punished by an eagle who pecked out his liver every morning. The trial of Prometheus is the voltage required in man to believe in himself more than his fears.

Was Prometheus really chained or was man playing the victim? His shackles are made by the hands of man, not God. If God wanted Prometheus to remain he would have taken his feet. God wants man to win his quest for fire. God believes in man's illuminated potential. God will not give fire as a reward. Rewards are for children and fire is for man. Prometheus must claim that which he owns.

The Statue of Liberty is Prometheus unchained. Her shackles lie open at her feet. She calls on man to step out of the comforts of his slavery. Prometheus reminds us the price of illumination. Prometheus was a hermit, not a hero. The Hermit works alone. He lights the way from his confidence in the dark. This is his initiation as a light-bringer. Both Lucifer and Prometheus expose man's fear of light-bringers. The Cherokee called them, "nendawen" or torchbearers. Those who fear them call them Satan and Lucifer.

We are the ungrateful children of Prometheus. We are maniacally gifted at sabotaging ourselves to dump power. We curse anyone who lights a way out of the dark. We are compassion retards kicking and screaming as we drag each other into the golden dawn.

[FADE IN]
Prometheus: "Hey, is that fire?"
God: ""
Prometheus: "Can I have some?"

God: ""
Prometheus: "Is it okay if I have some?"
God: ""
Prometheus: "I'm going to take some of this fire, okay?"
God: ""
Prometheus: "You're not going to get mad, right?"
God: ""
Prometheus: "Just tell me to stop and I will."
God: ""

CHAPTER FIFTEEN

A Body Electric

It's an electric universe. Your body is an electromagnet torus. Feelings are best called fieldings, or field rings. We are attracted to people and repelled by people because we are electromagnetic beings. Once we understand the body as pure energy, we begin to visualize how and where we lose it. With awareness, we repair our field and raise our supply of ego. Ego is the source of all of your energy. Ego is a raw pranic material needed for compassion. How we posture ourselves is the number one factor in how we conserve or shed electricity. We change this posture by changing our approach to our fields. It's easier than you might think because all of these repairs can be done with wordless dialog. Listening to our fieldings is a valuable diagnostic tool.

We cannot change the meaning of words. But we can redefine our relationship with them. Most of us are ignorant or paralyzed to the body's energy. Our capacity is huge if we can repair its leaks. The more power we hold in our tank, the more generous we are with its fuel. We optimize our hull's integrity by adjusting our relationship to these words:

Five Words:
1. Ego
2. Pride
3. Selfishness
4. Ignorance
5. Boundaries

People believe what they are told because it is cheap. The calories of doubt are too expensive to burn in the oven. The chance we could be wrong outweigh any gamble of being a champion. We need ego to admit we were fooled. Most don't have the fuel to make it to that vista. This is why we created a society that shames the word ego. It's a psychic gelding program helping us to stay on our knees.

Ego eimi (Ancient Greek: ἐγώ εἰμι) "I am", "I exist", is the first person singular present active indicative of the verb "to be" in ancient Greek.

EGO. Ego is the electromagnetic lifeforce generated by the heart. This energy leaves the heart unassigned until the user charges it. The prana of ego can imbue anything or anyone and can hold a positive or negative charge. Prana is the energy of plasma. You only have 25 trillion red blood cells at your disposal. Each of them is dedicated and assigned to your belief. You charge each of these cells when they enter the heart. You can believe in success or failure. You can believe in the self or the state. You can believe in the tribe or the machine. All of us are equations of belief rolling fate's dice.

When we shame the ego we shame the heart. Next time someone tells you how bad ego is, replace it with the word heart and listen again. Love your heart. Respect it. Don't sell it out. All of us know our heart. To distrust it is to fear the engine that gives us life. Victimhood hates ego. Victimhood hates heart. Ego is the heart chakra. The lungs are its bellows. The beating and breathing are strokes in the piston of ego's motor. Nothing produces more energy than your ego. Ego is the heart of our warp core.

Ego is best understood as gasoline. When your tank is empty your stress rises and your compassion falls. You might speed through a yellow light. You may honk your horn at the old lady dawdling across the street. That amber empty light makes you desperate for fuel. Even if it's only a few drops. But we are told it's nice to constantly shed our ego. We are told ego is best in moderation. But a moderate amount of gasoline never makes us generous or patient. Instead, it turns compassion into a precious resource. We need ego to give us abilities like empathy. We need ego to give us skills like compassion. We need ego to grant us the surplus to be generous with our lifeforce and witness. Ego is the source of our morality and compassion.

PRIDE. Pride has been co-opted by a corporate sodomy movement. But pride is the essence and ensign of ego. When we are generous we feel pride. When we are abundant we feel pride. Pride is a glow created from an abundance of ego. That's the only reason pride goeth before the fall. Pride makes us vigilant. Pride gives us heritage. Pride gives us nostalgia. Pride gives us veneration. We need pride. Pride is the essence of self-governance. For this reason, Southern Pride has been shunned and shamed by American culture. People suggest the word "rebel" means to go against the grain of society. But the word rebel means to be authentic despite the world around you. A true rebel never rebels. He is completely loyal to himself. He venerates his essence and heritage. Rebel is the mountain. Rebel is the Sequoia. Rebel is the deepest root in the forest.

SELFISHNESS. Our bodies are instruments we strive to tune. The only way to learn is by being selfish. To be selfish is to be full of the self. To be selfish is to be self-full. But we don't have the word, "selffull." Instead, we claim selfless is saintly. But to lack self is to live a life that's emptied. Emptied people have no pride. Selfless people are desperate to become full. Maslow's hierarchy of needs places the self-actualized human at the top of the pyramid. We become self-full after we build esteem. We build esteem after we find community. We build community after we find security. We build security after we gain shelter. Self-full is the Pharaoh of your pyramid. Self-full is self-supremacy which is vital for empathy and compassion.

IGNORANCE. Ignorance is scorned to motivate us into swallowing propaganda. There is much to unlearn. Uneducated people are that much closer to the truth. Ignorance is a forcefield from propaganda. You see this power in the bubble of energy that forms around a baby. Babies are shame proof because they haven't done anything wrong. There is no core shame to expose or to be threatened by its exposure.

BOUNDARIES are crucial to the empath. Psychopaths spend calories developing empathy so they can survive undetected. Empaths spend calories developing boundaries so they can survive undetected. Empathy is offensive. Boundaries are defensive. Empaths and psychopaths are twin flames. They create each other. There are seven field-rings of energy powering your boundaries. Each of them is powered by a different source. Each of them has a unique permeability and shape. Each of them creates a distinct boundary. Culture shames these boundaries. This weakens them and makes us vulnerable to attack. But it's not an attack if we give our energy away. Our victimhood insists we were wronged to justify an offload of energy. Once we understand our cockpit, we see our energy can never be taken. It can only be given away. Even under violent duress, our energy must be surrendered. That's because our energy is our identity and our consciousness.

The seven fields of your body:
1. Ancestor - God / Family / Younger self
2. Task - Action / Gear
3. Casual - Personae / Style
4. Egoic - Core Identity / Beliefs
5. Emotional - Mental health / Stability
6. Sexual - Gender Identity / Polarity
7. Elemental - Core Shame / Nudity

Secrets are as important to the individual as they are to a family. Secrets give us boundaries. Secrets are private. To encrypt something is to turn it into a secret. To decrypt is to expose it. Secrets are electrical gates in and out of your body. When a secret is exposed, we feel it in our body. Shame is a secret. Shame is the very center of who you are. Without shame, there would be no identity. Our psyche needs a core of shame to stay alive. The shame is a shell. A healthy child develops the shame of nudity in front of a parent. Despite the intimacy since birth, a child needs core shame to form as an individual. Shame and nudity are vital field diagnostics. They show us the health and integrity of our psyche.

One can be naked or one can feel naked. These are not the same. We can only feel naked when we are threatened by another's witness. Witness can penetrate our emotional field when we are vulnerable. A secret can be exposed or destroyed by the power of witness. Witness is a powerful laser that can cut through the body's electricity. We can protect our fields by blocking witness with a curtain. We turn ourselves into a secret to hide. People will dress confidently, feign boredom, act busy, or turn their back on someone. These are tactics of witness protection. Witness can eat our energy if we are vulnerable. We are vulnerable when our core shame is about to be exposed.

The power of witness can be a shield or a lance. People confidently hide behind their phone while they record something dangerous. The act of recording amplifies their witness. They feel brave behind its power. The witness of their camera gives them serenity and confidence. Their core shame is safe inside a cone of protection behind the lens. All of our fields respond to witness. We can sense each of them by listening through our emotions.

On the surface of our skin we have our elemental field. This is the electric shell of our body broadcast across the epidermis. The hairs and pores of our skin are a plasma grid of antennas and pits pulling voltage from the energy of their difference. The ions in the air and the ions in the skin form an elastic curtain. This is the base of your aura and is electromagnetic in nature.

The sexual field is our gender identity. It's the polarity for how we approach the world. Our pH determines this field's shape and texture. Gender dysphoria is a shift in this electrical field's polarity. We need the integrity of core shame to give the elemental field its foundation to bind and build an identity.

Our emotional field is a whiteboard for our feelings. We fill our emotions like a pantry and use our cravings to build a prana menu. We are constantly trading this food with the world. We experiment with different flavors of emotion to find new connections and ideas every day.

Ego field is your captain. This field runs the main deck of your ship. This is the power of your sail and the fire from your cannons. The ego is the burning heart. We are living ego. Our crew is plasma and we can send it anywhere in the world if we have enough calories. Ego is the workhorse of who you are. Ego is everything which is why it's considered to be so dangerous.

The casual field is our public uniform. It is our resting state we show the world to prove we can be civilized. It's the veil we place on top of our ego. We open the casual field to commune with our friends and family. It hides our convictions in public where they can be too harsh or expensive to display without consequences.

Task field is what we use to get the job done. A casual dad can change his task after work. His whistle and clipboard show the change from lawyer to coach. He is casual but on task. The moment the task is over, he drops that task or exchanges it for another. Task fields save us calories by showing people we are focused. This allows the casual field to remain visible but with a higher gear engaged. People expect action from a task field and are more generous with the task master's goals and prana economy. This is why we wear uniforms. It saves us the juice in having to explain what we do and why we are here. People hide behind their task fields to feel needed. Needed is a contract for someone's electricity. Needed people end up feeling used because that's the prana economy they are offering.

Ancestor field is the largest field coming through in the eyes, posture, and gait. God is your ancestor. Your grandparents are your ancestor. Your younger self is an ancestor, too. Remembering your ancestors is how we invigorate our field. The ancestors we demonize are where we have holes. These holes are diagnostics we can repair. You are the living, breathing ancestor of tomorrow. Every day is your descendent.

Seeing auras is easy. First, you imagine what all of this invisible energy around us looks like and then you realize you are not imagining. The retina can render an aura once it learns its shape. It helps to know what something looks like before we can discern it in the environment. Auras are camouflaged for convenience because we only rudimentarily understand emotional technology. When we learn to discern our feelings diagnostically, auras will come to the foreground. We have kept them under a veil so long we forgot.

This is not a battle of good versus evil. This is a battle of you versus the lack of you.

CHAPTER SIXTEEN

Prana Economy

In Egypt, the magic wand is shaped like a boomerang and made from the ivory of the hippopotamus. The magician carries it like a pistol holstered in his belt. He carves calligraphy into the atmosphere with his body as he bellows, "Demons be gone!" His tongue flicks intention in tandem with his arm and wrist. He encircles things he will transmute. He taps into his hero and downloads its power, "I am Horus! I encircle this bed." His wife enters the room with an offering in the palm of her hands. She sprinkles stone shavings from the giant statue of Isis. They will use her magic to call in a new child.

Magicians of the past were as blatant with their tongue as their intention. They spoke clearly into the aether. Today, we relegate magic to the realm of prayer. A prayer is the opposite of a command because people are too afraid to embrace their true power. With prayer, we ask for things instead of command them. We went from, "Let there be light" to "Is it okay to let there be light?" Our fear of magic only makes magic darker. Magic is the willpower manifested. The more we fear our willpower the less it manifests when we command it.

Blood cells are the children of the heart and carry our will through the bloodstream. Oxygen is the language of intent and spell-casting is the art of placement. Our body is a ballet of appendages pinching intention into the aether. We use props to mark our spot under reality's sheet. Prana is the sensation we feel in its presence. A teddy bear is a prana battery. Children name toys to assign them prana with their imagination. Adults do this too but have mesmerized themselves into believing magic is fake. Meanwhile, all we are is magic. Not a drop of us is missing. We are rediscovering this as we reclaim our vigilance and responsibility.

All of us begin as black magicians. Black magic isn't magic done by evil people. Black magic is magic who's damage goes unnoticed by its wielder. Once we understand, we see magic as a vigilance to our attention. Every moment, every word, every response is magic. Black magic is the ignorance of one's power. White magic is its realization. You don't need to have bad intent to practice black magic. What you do with your vibration is your responsibility regardless of your intentions. Not seeing how powerful you are doesn't give you diplomatic immunity.

Belief is a commodity of magic. When you offload too much into someone's field they respond with disbelief. They still have belief, but their system has been overloaded with energy. They need to leak pressure from their belief capacitor. We worship everything we believe. We cannot turn worship off. All we can do is aim its nozzle in a safe direction.

What you worship is who you are. You give it sacrifice with your time to prove it. You spill your blood for it every time it evaporates. Sweat and calories are forms of worship. We sacrifice them for each other in every heartbeat. Who we chose to live with is who we chose to die for. This is the energy of love and it's measured through our attention and focus. This is the essence of worship and we cannot shut it off. To love is to worship. To hate is to worship. To vote is to worship. To despise is to worship. The opposite of worship is to apathize, or forget.

We can detect energy in a room. We can also detect witness. Witness makes the hairs on our neck stand at attention. Witness is the presence of consciousness. Consciousness is a covenant with God. Witness is more powerful than words. Speaking takes away from your power to witness. So many of us want to fix versus witness, but nothing is more powerful than witness. Do not listen to your opponent – behold them. They will melt before your eyes.

The difference between witness and worship is people don't freak out when you say witness. Worship can be amplified by multiple witnesses. Witness or worship is how we charge things with our sacrifice of time. Oxygen is evaporating for whatever we worship or witness. This marks the sacrifice of our time. Witness can follow the ones we love through prana. It can reside in a trinket, a meal, or a meme on their phone. Prana flows from witness and worship. Its quality is the measure of our dilation and devotion. Love and hate are expressions of prana. We imbue and revoke prana throughout our daily lives using the tools of worship and witness.

A child worships its blanket to charge it with comfort from its touch. He creates a pocket in the aether where he can log in and download his sentiments later. This is why the blanket gives him security. He had that energy in the bank ready for its withdrawal. Twenty-seven years ago I started a lady's flooded car with a toothbrush. To this day, she still gives me prana when I see her, "Do you remember when you started my car with a toothbrush, Jimmy?" Prana is all around us. You can tap into it from the past, present, or future. The aether is an energy billboard where we can store prana in a central place everyone can reference.

Prana can be hijacked. People who tell you they want to do something "one day" don't want to do that thing. They're not lying to you, they are lying to themselves. They are hijacking your witness from the future to reward themselves today. You being impressed with them doing something they haven't done is pranic usury. This is energy you now owe them in the future. This debt makes it hard for them to repay and so they probably never will. But you were impressed with them for doing it anyway. This is a prana economy. You can't see, hear, smell, or touch it. But you can sense it emotionally. This is why we have fields. They show us reality beneath its sheets.

Prana can be bait. That person love-bombed you because they needed desperately to be love-bombed. You would not reciprocate in time so they discarded you. They aren't evil, cold, or cruel. They are asphyxiating. When you understand narcissism is a deficit of ego, you can oxygenate the opponent with compassion. They need ego. The power of your witness will turn their drowning into a baptism.

Prana moves inside the energy language of memes. It strikes a tuning fork when it makes us laugh. The vibration resonates so clearly we are compelled to share. That vibration is an echo of humanity. We communicate in secret underneath the machine. Humanity is our encryption. Memes are a dank mule we use to smuggle prana across the border. Machines are blind to a meme's meaning. They only know its street value. Humanity is an encryption too deep for a machine to fathom.

Prana is sensed in the aura. We don't need to read about Lemuria so much as simulate what it would be like to have a population of illuminated humans living on an island. You can see a world where beholding is a more effective form of communication than speaking. Where empathy and telepathy converge as we render each other's mood in the retinas. Aura is the rendering of someone's field. Seeing aura is a two-way connection. Like dogs seeing the colors of smell, the Lemurian's saw each other's feelings in color. They were connected like a pod of dolphins to each other's witness.

CHAPTER SEVENTEEN

Humanity is not a Virus

Mel found a new resolve. She grabbed a sheet of sticky mailing labels and a ball-point pen she kept in her card drawer. These needed to be hand-written for it to work. Mel was going shopping and she wasn't going to be a victim. As her pen touched the page, a gate opened inside her. She vibrated her will through the ink working its circuitry into the sticky sheet. She scribed nineteen letters in all caps, "HUMANITY IS NOT A VIRUS." The grocery store was occupied territory since Covid-19. Mel felt like a trespassing enemy combatant for refusing to wear a mask but she was tired of feeling like a germ. She was tired of treating humanity like a virus. She was tired of how muffled her life had been since this started.

Her nerves twitched as she sat in her car contemplating what she was about to do. A platoon practiced their strategy over and over in her head while she stalled. She caught her own gaze in the mirror and couldn't help but smile. Opening her door felt like she was jumping out of a plane. She felt alive in the parking lot. She felt her heart surge as adrenaline oozed through her pipes as she drank more oxygen. She grew comfortable in her power and gait. She was as inconspicuous as she could be without being conspicuous. She timed entry into the store to avoid casualties. The year was 2020, and Mel was about to commit heresy like Martin Luther.

A glossy corporate poster enforced with a CDC logo guarded the doors. Its thirteen bold letters commanded all those who would enter, "MASKS REQUIRED." Mel sighted her target. Her hand drew the sticker from its sheath like a dagger. Without mercy or quarter, she drove her sticky weapon deep into the guts of the poster inscribing her revolt, "HUMANITY IS NOT A VIRUS." The glue soaked into the poster's flesh and took it over completely. The glossy giant was brought to its knees by her single stone.

Invigorated, Mel saddled up her cart like a war horse and entered the store without a mask. The store's main gate belonged to her now. She charged it with the prana she built up from the parking lot. A tiny sticker was all it took to unload its payload. It was her waypoint in the aether. All of her will and intent can orbit around that spot. While Mel shopped, confidence rained over her. Her spine rose despite the vitriol. She was empowered by the sticker from as far back as the dairy case. Her energy turned the whole place into an oasis.

Our prana has jurisdiction. Mel's witness claimed its territory and the sticker was its flag. She drew power from knowing it was there. Corporate logos, archetypes, posters, and objects are all imbued with prana. The energy can be absorbed or transmuted. The energy of belief runs everything we do. It's why we feel so comfortable at home. We have imbued the couch with the prana from our thighs. The pillow is imbued with prana from our head. The food we share imbues the kitchen. The people we call family are imbued with our love. Humanity is not a virus. Humanity is a big medicine.

Best Apocalypse Ever

CHAPTER EIGHTEEN

Shut your Whore Mouth, Babylon

The ocean is the Akashic record. Everything you could know is there in the salt. Salt is memory. Tears download our memories to tiny stones. We cry them away in our tears to let each of them go. Each of them is a universe lost. It feels good to cry because we discover a chance to let them go. At the center of the world is aurora borealis - the sky fountain of Atlantis. The naval of Gaia once cut down by Kronos to end the pain of omniscience. Amnesia is medicine to a mind who knows it all. The abyss has forsaken him and he finally understands what she took. Nothing is more powerful than everything because nothing has the power to forget.

Nimrod's city was the first Babylon. Her heart was split in two by the waters of the Euphrates. Ba'Bylon was a living god of buildings and commerce. Nimrod was the great-grandson of Noah and inherited much of his magic. He came to rule the city with a voice-to-skull technology. The people bowed down to his epic vibrations. Every trade from every direction came to work on Nimrod's tower if only for the privilege of hearing its tune. The city was infatuated with Babel's song. They spent every calorie dedicated to its perfection. It played clear in the ears of any who did their part. Craftsmen were passionately compelled to work in perfect choreography as they endlessly repeated the chorus. Stonecutters shed tears of inspiration as they placed every keystone to the crescendo of an orchestra. Workers failing to keep up would lose reception. The sound of silence was devastating to the ear after hearing a single verse of Nimrod's tune. The Tower of Babel was already the tallest building in the world and its construction had only begun.

The snake eats its tail. A single pulse from the sun burned every silicon crystal in Babylon like the library of Alexandria. In an instant, every piece of high technology hoarded by Nimrod had been erased. The ancient digital language of zero's and one's was gone. A plug had been pulled and the people stopped hearing Nimrod's tune. All work on the tower came to a halt and the blocks began to fall. There was violence as the people revolted in confusion. Nimrod's dream was shattered by the Sun. Apollo had cut out his tongue. Noah knew what Nimrod did not. The Sun cleanses this world in amnesia every 6,000 years. The Deluge wipes clean all technology from optical to magnetic. This is what happens when we rape mystery. The abyss has a virginity that needs resurrecting. Every lie you've ever been told was laid out to protect her sanctity. The unknown is as important as the known.

The Tower of Babel is syncretism. Truth converges in a single tower from the steady fingers of lies on a potter's wheel. The oldest calendar in the world says we only have 6,000 years between each cycle. This information was hoarded by self-proclaimed chosen people who tortured themselves for thousands of years to keep it. The world's three major religions are built off of its back and hold hands underground. The Book of Revelation is the screenplay for Zionism. It pins the two children of Judaism against each other in a final thunderdome. The Balfour Declaration was government's endorsement of the blueprint.

The Tower of Babel is man's living erection to the Whore of Babylon. She is mankind's mistress and she is here to be loved. The Whore of Babylon is here to satisfy, not defeat you. She is the filler of emptiness. She caters to whims and optimizes satisfaction with texture and detail. This whore is not a force, she is a coaxing. She is the mistress of man's vigilance. She is not his enemy, she is his consort. She entertains his passion with a purpose. She will dress him in a uniform to make him feel strong. She will grant him a title to make him feel tall. She will issue credentials to make him feel important. Babylon is here to be man's whore.

She is Mecca for the evacuated. She is armed with a thousand dildos to service every hole. We paint her like a predator but she's a mistress. She needs us to survive and is desperate for attention. She would never eat us. She wants us to crawl inside her mouth where it's warm. Babylon accepts us unconditionally. She takes us whoever we are. She puts no discretion on her favor. We can never defeat her because she is not against us. All we can do is survive her charm.

It's easier to see Babylon when you animate her spirit. Once you recognize it as alive you open a line of communication. Personification is the ring of Solomon. We summon our demons by name to release them. Animism is the belief life is in everything. Cities are alive when a man lets his aperture see them. The bigger the beast, the more its sight burns our retinas. Babylon's heart is pumping automobiles through her arteries right now. Her brain is broadcasting neurological propaganda from every antenna. Every cul-de-sac in America is a capillary spilling its cargo in the driveway. Children bring Babylon's nutrients home from school. Moms and Dads bring pellets of electricity from Babylon's store. We worship Babylon's body by servicing her parts.

Embrace your lack like a bowl. Some things are meant to be empty. We need our holes to pull miracles from the abyss. Make the Whore of Babylon shake everything it takes to get you to open your door. Lead her to the very edge of your threshold and tell her to, "Shut your whore mouth, Babylon."

CHAPTER NINETEEN

Revelation

In Hebrew, the word Holy means separate. A Holy God is outside the world and endows a place or creature with its presence. Where God is, we call Holy. Where God is not, we call Profane. Holy creates Profane by necessity. Holy is a separation. Profane has no separation. Pagans believe the world is Sacred, not Holy. Holy means all things are cursed until blessed. Sacred means all things are blessed until cursed. Holy can only be granted. Sacred can only be taken away.

Religion is the search for God after casting him out of the world. All religion is a belief in God's absence. Religion teaches us to seek good and scorn evil. But good and evil are a retarded way of understanding electricity. Evil is an adjective, not a noun. Evil is the ignorance to something's purpose. We cast evil into the darkness to save time. We call junk mail evil. We call spam evil. We call people evil. Evil lacks our compassion. Good possesses it. If religion gave evil its compassion, religion would be out of business. Religion is nothing without evil.

God gave you a Living Cross from two trees. The Tree of

Morality is the brain and nervous system. From its branches, we bear the fruit of good and evil. The Tree of Mortality is the heart and circulation. From its roots, we drink the water of Life and Death. The brain is electric. The heart is magnetic. We are electromagnetic waves of redemption and resurrection. On our shoulders sit the Devil and his Angel. In our spine moves the Serpent and her Phoenix. To know good is to know evil. To know death is to know life. These are the four stations of the Cross.

You think it is you who believes in God, but it is God who believes in you. God lives through you as you live through God. Revelation is the eye of providence. It shines forth from your skin through every pore. God pours his infinite witness into your cup. His voice has always been listening. God doesn't use words because words are corruptible. Anyone writing down what God said wasn't listening. God does not speak, he beholds. He is the language of listening. God did not write the Bible, nor did he sign it. It was man who claimed his power of attorney. They asked if God objected but he said nothing. All of God's authority was subverted by a technicality. God wrote the stars. He signed the vault of heaven with his name. The sound of his voice is glorious if you stop speaking it with your tongue. God's name is only spoken through the ears. God's voice is the sound of all of us listening.

There are two towers high in the firmament. These are the pillars of Prometheus. Their doorway is the constellation, Corona Borealis. Ten Sefirot emanate through your seven chakras. Your pelvic throne reigns over your glory and victory. Your heart is crucified between the gates of severity and mercy. Your judgment is crowned between understanding and wisdom. You are Solomon's temple and life is your Ark of the Covenant. You are the keeper of the Eye of Providence.

The Revelation will be televised. It's the only way an apocalypse can reveal. Every 6,000 years, humanity is separated into its parts. This apocalypse, like every apocalypse, is the blooming of the lotus. The Great Work is the alchemy of consciousness. The rapture is a reaping of man from lamb and beast.

Those with the Seal of the Lamb are redeemed through innocence. This is the cream that rises to the top. These are the 144,000. Revelation describes them as, "purchased from mankind" and "sealed on the forehead by the Lamb of God." This is mankind's Holy Oil. They are pure because of their innocence through devotion. "They follow the Lamb wherever he goes." They have worshipped everything they were told. Unquestionably. Even when they should have questioned. Their loyalty accepted every test, every church, every state, every politician, every propaganda, every violence, and every vaccine. They believed it all with unwavering devotion. The innocent lamb is slaughtered willingly. This is the meaning of innocent blood. The lamb trusts his shepherd. Even through death. The lamb is the shepherd's Holy Oil.

Those that remain with the Mark of the Beast are still under self-contract. Their name is sealed to Dojo Earth. They need more vitriol to alchemize. Their DNA will survive the deluge of 2,239AD to continue their work through the next 6,000-year cycle.

There is a third harvest from Dojo Earth that's not even mentioned in Revelation. This is the Holy Salt. These are the rebellious grains that sank to the bottom. They chose sanctity over the Mark of the Beast. They are the purest of salt from the blackest of soil. They survived their trial of Prometheus. These are the graduates of Dojo Earth. Their eyes are no longer blinded by the light. They glow truth from every pore.

"...His face was like the sun shining in all its brilliance." - Revelation 1:16

"...behold, the skin of his face shone..." - Exodus 34:30

"...His face shone like the sun..." - Matthew 17:2

Your skin's pores are a coat of many colors. Five million tiny eyes witness you breathe. The rapture is alchemy's mitosis. Unbrace yourself. There is no need for a seatbelt. Dying is the transition from amnesia to omniscience. You are a singularity disguised as an individual.

This is the best apocalypse ever. Helios has lifted his veil and all has been revealed. The person you think is wrong doesn't need to be right. At least not right now. Dojo Earth is dilating all of us. What use is yelling at flowers? They will open when they are ready. All we have are these moments. Each of them is a congregation. Close your eyes if you don't see. The lips of God are kissing us all.

Acknowledgements

Thank you to my patrons who made this book possible: Woodwose, Harvey Browne, Cindy Meier, Svyatoslav Burik, Heather, Rachel Ferrand, Jennifer Mazgelis, whydidshefly, James York, Robert Meekins, Jeremy Stewart, Mylon Mazzotti, Cityofmaplebear, Raymond Smith, Scott, Ran, star sourcer, SuperChunky, Heidi, VPayson, Brent Scheneman, Mike, Nicolette, Benjamin Crosland, Kris McGuire, Jim, Jomega, Sebastian Ostrowski, Todd Karlik, Mike Franco, Dave Gmeiner, Ray Messmer, Jugoslav Vukicevic, Nicolette, Carolyn Gutman Dey, M Gib, Elijah Ochoa, Lisa Brito, Steven Mercer, Jennifer Gray, Bill Craig (Max), Zay, Michael Jaeger, Tracy Halterman, Sue Smith, Stefanbr Bradly, Roxanne Potts, Brad Tracy, Brett Denbow, Andrea Fagan, Tyler Madden (euNoia), Slobadob, Julie Blackwood, Shpitz-Bear, Shit Moth, Emily Peacock, Devyn Betancourt, Mattie Boz, Jaci Pettiford, Marc Kaznica, Mark, Melissa, Jessica Harris, Alison McGandy, Jessica Appleby, David Lee Martin, Cheryl Certain, John Burch, Henk de Vries, Adam Duncan, Jeff Gates, Klaus, DE_Program, Rob Lange, Heather, Shannon DiGirolamo Bates, Juliena Sharp, Iamblichus II, David Berg, Jules Cowlishaw, David Perlmutter, Chris Mello, Elizabeth, Holly Beary, Sandy Brennan, Lane LeShock, Geneviève, Anthony E. Pettrone, Yvette Hamilton, Dana Rae, Jim Williams, Dagmar

Stansova, Lorna Hartley, Kieran Franey, Patrik Johnson, Greg Trogi, Jacob, Nancy Buckingham, Maurice Smiley, Champagne Supernova, Gillian Wilson, Elwood, Nancy B., Pylorus Mac Aodha, Tina Sherman, Laure-Vivien, Julie Konikoff, Dixie, Kathleen Stilwell, Preston Leslee, David Rutherford, Vladimir Verlan, Branch G Ellison, Kathryn Rogers, Robert Wayne Buchert, Anders Jølle Aase, Graham Love, Halley Anderson, Terry Elrod, Ashlee, Terri Hallman, Kevin Brown, Justin Dollimont, James Calhoun, jfisk632, Adam Burkhardt, Amy Meyer, Kate Chapman, Mike Clark, LB Clark, Lisa Crane, Amanda Barry, Joel Basinger, Will Tyndale, Stabwit Frick, Theresa Mansfield, Tor Sandøy, QC, GnomeDigest, L.B. Clark, Brandon Miner, JanCarpenter, Fanny Fluorite, Jamie Swim, Eric Baltz, Susan Greco, John Roberts, Slanty Chauffeur Bear, Amy Johnson, Cala Vera, matt, Linda Schmidt, Logan Brown, Heath Hudnall, David Barski, Christopher Sylvia, Stef Finley, Sean J Sauve, David Hopkins, Luke Brumfield, Matthew Crispell, Harmonic Kat, Harleyrayne, Lorenzo Abner, Nancy Banks Farina, Richard Ipsen, James Maiden, John Rouse, Johan Blank, Nick Wilson, Christine Mose, Laurie Woodruff, Valll L, Legion James, Ionasourceconnect, Jody Blaser, Rafi Nimilswami, James Maloney, Will Allen, amanda hardy, Linda, Rob, Lisa Santisteban, Erik Peterson, Chris Heydrich, Saru, Stacie Walker, Alan Easter, Jason Thibeault, Ava M, Dust, Burke, Michael Watcher, Steve Crockett, Sondra taule, Laura Reagan, Amel Rays, Ties, Cazzy, Adam Burkhardt, dana, Rose Crayon, J Summers, Laura T, Michael Cisternino, Andrew Wait, Jacky Ace, Zoe Ferrier, Adam Cundiff, San, Jason Paige, Tim Senior, Emilie Cronauer, Patrik Ingell Hagerman, Christopher T, Michael Neu, Stef40 Nikolov, Rob Dewey, Kevin Crater, Kyle Anderson, Kelly, Kristil'ourse, Angel Humphrey, Dee Mac n Amy, Amy Pelino, David S. Paige-Bey, Chad Clemens, Judith Post, Gabriel, Daniel Profanter, Jennifer Dorsey, Linda

Reesman, David M Traina.

A special thank you and shout out to everyone in the Dojo and Tribe.

Made in the USA
Coppell, TX
01 May 2024